Brady Denial?

You CAN Get Your Guns Back!

C.E. Hill, Attorney-at-Law

Paladin Press • Boulder, Colorado

DEPARTMENT OF THE TREASURY
BUREAU OF ALCOHOL, TOBACCO AND FIREARMS
FIREARMS TRANSACTION RECORD PART I - OVER-THE-COUNTER

WARNING: You may not receive a firearm if prohibited by Federal or State Law. The information
whether you are prohibited under law from receiving a firearm. Read the Important Notices, Instructions and Definition
Prepare in original only. All entries must be in ink.

Section A - Must Be Completed Personally By Transferee

1. Transferee's Full Name (Last, First, Middle)

atrick Henry

2. Residence Address (No., Street, City
office box)

1776 Freedom St.
Lexington, MA

5. ☒ Male
   ☐ Female

6. Birth Date
Month ____

3. Place of Birth
foreign count

Concord,

DENIED

8. Race (Ethnicity) (Check one or more bo
   ☐ American Indian or Alaska Native
   ☐ Hispanic or Latino

9. What is your State of residence (if any)?
   State of residence only if you have resided in a State for at least 90 days prior t

What is your country of citizenship? (List more than one, if applicable.)

a citizen of the United States, what is your INS-issued alien nu

Certification Of

by writing "yes" or "no" in the boxes to
listed on this form? **Warning**
you are not the act
and examples

Brady Denial? You CAN Get Your Guns Back!
by C.E. Hill, Attorney-at-Law

Copyright © 2005 by Cindy Ellen Hill

ISBN 10: 1-58160-478-5
ISBN 13: 978-1-58160-478-8
Printed in the United States of America

Published by Paladin Press, a division of
Paladin Enterprises, Inc.
Gunbarrel Tech Center
7077 Winchester Circle
Boulder, Colorado 80301 USA
+1.303.443.7250

Direct inquiries and/or orders to the above address.

PALADIN, PALADIN PRESS, and the "horse head" design
are trademarks belonging to Paladin Enterprises and
registered in United States Patent and Trademark Office.

Visit our Web site at www.paladin-press.com

Contents

V

To my girls, Emma, Julie, and Evelyn.
In your generation's hands lies the future of our rights
and civil liberties; guard them with vigilance and courage.

Introduction

As a gun-owning lawyer, I get calls every day from people who have received erroneous Brady denials or, worse, Brady denials based on dumb incidents that happened so long ago the person barely remembers what happened. How many of us recall the details of everything we did in 1972?

I've been able to help dozens of these folks restore their firearms rights. I've helped people get copies of documents to correct their criminal records; gone back into court decades after a conviction to get the terms of the charge amended; and spent hours in dusty library basements (and getting clerks in distant states to spend hours in their dusty library basements) researching exactly what a statute said at the time someone was convicted under it in 1962. Not everyone's firearms rights can be restored, but if there is a way, it brings me great joy to see the Bureau of Alcohol, Tobacco, Firearms, and Explosives (ATF) hand back someone's seized firearms collection.

Countless firearms owners and lawyers ask me about the impact of various convictions on firearms rights and seek my advice on getting their guns back; this book assembles the answers to those questions. The information in here is useful for gun owners or prospective gun owners who aren't sure if they'll get a Brady denial; for anyone who has already gotten a Brady denial and wants to understand it or, better yet, do something about it; and for criminal defense and firearms lawyers seeking to advise their clients regarding criminal charges or the reinstatement of their valuable rights.

1

Our right to bear arms is a precious part of our national heritage, culture, and law. A Brady denial—tantamount to a determination that your right to bear arms has been extinguished—should not be taken lightly. Correcting an erroneous record or having the reason for the denial overturned or removed is your right. You may well be able to get your guns back, and this book will show you how.

1

Denied!

PORTRAIT OF A BRADY DENIAL

You belly up to the counter at the local gun shop, a wad of cash in one hand and a pen in the other, finally coming to claim that beautiful chunk of steel you've been looking at for years. You fill out the ATF form and hand over your photo ID. You then regale your buddies with tales of all the deer/pigeons/targets you're planning on hitting, while the gun dealer makes the phone call to the state POC (point of contact) or federal NICS (National Instant Check System) Brady background check number. At the other end of the line, an operator takes the information and runs your name through more than three million records of criminal convictions, warrant lists, domestic stay-away orders, military discharge indexes, and mental health files, attempting to determine if you meet one of nine different criteria that would make you a person prohibited from purchasing a firearm under federal law.

Minutes later, the gun dealer slides your ID back over the counter to you. As you pick it up, you notice it's sitting on top of a brochure outlining your rights if you receive a Brady denial. You look up. His face is grim. The place goes quiet. Finally someone makes an uncomfortable wisecrack. "What'd ya do, beat up the old lady?" or "Jeez, you rob a bank or something?"

You're incredulous. "Why?" you ask. The gun dealer crosses his arms, defensive now. "Couldn't tell you," he says.

The room suddenly tense, you stride outside, overwhelmed by visions of yourself sitting home alone while your friends are all out on hunting trips or at the shooting range. "Will I ever get that new rifle?" you think, then get hit with a wave of anxiety: What about all the guns you already have at home?

I GOT DENIED—NOW WHAT?

Getting a Brady denial is not necessarily the end of the road for your firearms rights. Depending on the reason you got a denial and some other factors in your life history, it is possible to restore your firearms rights through appeal, correction of erroneous records, or by expungement, pardon, or retroactive amendment of the underlying disqualifying incident.

The Brady Handgun Violence Prevention Act of 1993, 18 U.S.C. Section 922(t), is named for former White House Press Secretary James S. Brady, who was shot during the 1981 assassination attempt on President Ronald Reagan and suffered permanent disabilities. The act originally required local law enforcement officers to conduct background checks on everyone who attempted to purchase a handgun from a federally licensed firearms dealer (FFL). In November 1998, this so-called handgun statute was amended to include all long gun purchases; and now the background checks are processed through the NICS system or, with federal approval, through a state POC. If these "Brady checks" come back with a denial, it means the FFL cannot sell the firearm to the purchaser.

From the beginning of the NICS system through 2002, more than 35 million Brady checks were performed in NICS states, and nearly that many again in POC states.[1] Brady denials under NICS have run a steady 2 percent per year. Because POC states have different record-keeping systems, it is difficult to determine the state denial rate, but it likely averages close to the NICS state rate.

Of the roughly 62,000 Brady denials per year in those states where NICS does the Brady checks, only about 10,000—around 15 percent—are appealed. Of this 15 percent who appeal, almost a third—3,000 per year—get their denial overturned and their firearms rights restored. Additional firearms owners get their rights

4

restored through other channels besides the Brady appeal, such as having their records corrected by their state records agency or by having their criminal convictions pardoned or expunged.

Extrapolating from these figures, it is reasonable to think that another 20,000 people per year who receive Brady denials could restore their firearms rights if they chose to try.

It may be that a few of the other 85 percent of people who receive Brady denials—more than 50,000 Americans a year—may have believed that an appeal in their case would be futile because of unpleasant facts involved or other personal circumstances. But most people who don't appeal their Brady denials make that choice based on lack of information, lack of money to hire a lawyer or investigator to assist them, or out of fear of drawing further unwanted attention from federal and state law enforcement authorities.

The devil of restoring firearms rights after a Brady denial is in the details. The precise nature of the disqualification and your life history since the disqualifying incident will be key to determining the odds of success in restoring your firearms rights. This book will walk you through the process of determining whether you are one of the 20,000 people per year who ought to have their firearms back.

THIS CAN'T BE RIGHT!

Getting a Brady denial usually comes as a shock, and with it comes embarrassment and confusion. The person involved often has no idea why he was denied. [Editor's note: For grammatical simplicity, we'll use the masculine pronoun throughout the book. No gender bias is intended.] Sometimes he may have a prior criminal conviction but be unaware that it's the kind of conviction that impacts firearms rights—very few people who know that they have a felony conviction on their records try to purchase a firearm from a legal firearms dealer. (I did have one surreal conversation with a guy who had killed someone with a knife and didn't understand why he got a Brady denial since his murder conviction had nothing to do with a firearm. I suspect that this conversation was one in a billion.)

Most denied applicants are unaware that they are prohibited persons under federal law either because they weren't aware of the many different categories of disqualification, or because they didn't think the disqualifications applied to them.

Common causes of surprise include:

- Matters that occurred when the applicant was a juvenile but were adjudicated as adult cases.
- Felony convictions that resulted in a fine or probation only (the federal definition doesn't require you serve jail time to be disqualified), especially property crimes, such as stealing a lawn ornament or tires.
- Criminal charges that occurred in the distant past (all federal firearms prohibitions apply to all convictions no matter how long ago they occurred).
- Misdemeanor convictions for disorderly conduct, simple assault, and violations of abuse prevention orders, in which the case involved a family member or person sharing living quarters (the federal definition of misdemeanor crime of domestic violence doesn't specify what the crime has to be called and includes anyone sharing a household, not just romantic partners or family members).

According to NICS, most erroneous Brady denials are due to criminal record errors. Some of the most common criminal history mistakes that lead to Brady denials include:

- Confusion of criminal history with that of a twin, other sibling, or a person with a similar name, address, or Social Security number. (If you have twins, make sure they don't get sequential Social Security numbers!)
- Record does not reflect that a felony charge was amended to a misdemeanor charge before conviction.
- Record fails to note that a matter has been dismissed, expunged or pardoned, or was a juvenile case.
- Misinterpretation where matter that was a misdemeanor at the time of conviction has since been changed to a felony. This is increasingly common as our criminal laws get ever more punitive.
- Difficulty interpreting record entries from other states,

6

which vary widely (for example, misinterpreting Florida misdemeanor convictions as felonies due to the letters FL in the docket number).

WHAT DOES A BRADY DENIAL MEAN?

Receiving a Brady denial means your records on file at that National Criminal Information Center show you to be a person prohibited from possessing firearms under federal or state law. This means you are not only prevented from purchasing the gun you submitted the Brady check for, but you are also prohibited from possessing all the firearms you already own, even those you got prior to adoption of the Brady Act. Since Brady denials are reported to law enforcement agencies for the purpose of seizing your guns or having you charged with illegal firearms possession, it is wise to remove your firearms from your possession while you are appealing your Brady denial.

"Possession" means that the firearm is accessible to you and it is not necessarily the same thing as "ownership." Federal law can prohibit you from "possessing" firearms, but you are still allowed to "own" them. Think of it this way: If you rack up too many points for speeding, you may lose your driver's license and be prohibited from driving; however, you are still allowed to own a car. You can still let other licensed drivers use your car or you can sell it if you need the cash.

Federal firearms laws goes a little further than this. If you are a prohibited person, your guns cannot be kept where you have access to them. In our car example, this would be like saying that you can still keep the title and registration in your bureau drawer, but you have to get the car out of your yard and surrender your keys. You still have the right to sell the car, whether it's for scrap or for another driver to use, and you have the right to store it somewhere else so that it will be available to you when you get your license back.

If you get a Brady denial, promptly place your firearms in the possession of a family member, friend, or FFL outside your household or business. This person should be aware of your Brady denial and agree to maintain possession of the firearms until your Brady denial is resolved. ATF may ask that the person put this statement in writing. If your Brady denial is overturned, you can get your guns back into your possession. If it turns out that you are permanently prohibited from possessing firearms, you can still have the firearms sold for cash, or trade, or give them away, provided that you do not bring them back into your personal possession.

If you keep your firearms in your possession after receiving a Brady denial, law enforcement officers may get a warrant and legally seize your firearms and, after a short forfeiture process, destroy them. If this happens, you will not get your guns back, and you will not receive any compensation for them. Firearms owners often don't want to admit defeat or "surrender" by giving up their guns, even to a friend or relative, while they fight their Brady denial. Give careful consideration to this decision, especially if you have either an investment gun collection or guns with strong sentimental value, like Dad's service pistol or Grandpa's shotgun that you are waiting to pass down to your kids. Set your pride aside and get these firearms into safe, lawful hands temporarily so that you don't lose them forever.

WHAT HAPPENS TO SEIZED GUNS?

The ATF has the power to seize any firearm or other property for forfeiture when that firearm or property has been involved, used, or intended to be used in violation of federal law. 27 CFR Section 72.21(a). This includes firearms that are in the possession of a person who is prohibited from possessing them. Once the firearms are seized, ATF has to start legal forfeiture proceedings within 120 days. 27 CFR Section 72.21(b).

If the value of the firearms seized from you is less than $100,000, ATF can proceed by a summary forfeiture process. The bureau must publish a notice once a week for three weeks in some newspaper within the judicial district where the seizure was made. This notice must note that anyone wanting to make a claim on the seized property by filing a petition with ATF must do so within 30 days of the last notice. *Thirty-one days after the last newspaper notice, ATF can proceed to destroy the firearms.* However, if they take longer (as they sometimes do for logistical reasons), ATF can act on any petition that comes in until the firearms are destroyed. All seized guns are supposed to be destroyed, rather than sold at auction like other forfeited property, in accordance with federal statute. 18 U.S.C. Section 924(d).

If the value of the firearms seized is more than $100,000, the chief attorney for ATF will set a special process for having the collection appraised and posted, and you will have a longer period of time in which to make a petition to reclaim the guns.

The ATF can proceed with forfeiture and destroy your guns even if the government does not charge you with a crime, or if the government charges you with a crime and then drops the charges, as long as there is "clear and convincing evidence" that you held the guns illegally. 18 U.S.C. Section 924(d)(1). However, if charges proceed and you are either acquitted, or the charges are dropped on the motion of the defense, or if your guns were seized due to a family court temporary restraining order and the order then expires or is rescinded, ATF must return your guns to you or someone you designate, unless it is illegal for you to have the guns in your possession.

9

While this would seem to imply that ATF will wait to see what happens to your case before disposing of the guns, this isn't necessarily so, although in most cases the seized firearms will be held as evidence in the case against you. Still, it usually makes sense to file the petition seeking to claim the seized firearms, just to be sure. Always consult with your attorney on this point, however; sometimes in order to file a claim petition protesting the forfeiture, you would have to admit things that would be harmful to you in your criminal defense case, so you may wind up making a difficult choice between fighting forfeiture or defending the criminal charges.

There are even some provisions allowing for attorney's fees if you successfully fight the forfeiture, although Congress has the ability to limit the money available for these payments in their appropriations to ATF.

WHAT ABOUT MY WIFE'S AND KID'S GUNS?

Firearms owned by other people in your household are a big gray area in the law. Last time I checked, women in America were allowed to own property independently of their husbands. (They even let us vote now, too.) So if the man of the house gets a Brady denial, does the woman of the house have to give up her gun?

This question also comes down to the tricky issue of "possession." If the firearm is kept in a nightstand drawer next to the couple's bed where the husband could, if he so chose, get ahold of it, then the gun meets the definition of being in his possession even though he doesn't own it.

It is up to the firearm's owner to ensure that the prohibited person does not have access to the firearm. This could include locking the firearm in a gun safe that the prohibited person doesn't have the combination to whenever that person is at home, or it could mean removing the gun—or the prohibited person—from the household unless or until the Brady denial gets reversed.

The situation with firearms belonging to children under 18 is worse than that of spouses because in most states children under 18 can't legally own firearms. So although you may have bought a deer rifle or shotgun for junior for Christmas, legally speaking it probably is owned by the adult who purchased it.

A separate gun safe for the spouse's or children's guns, provided that the person with the Brady denial does not have the key or combination, may be enough in many circumstances to allow the rest of the family to keep their guns. However, there is no cut-and-dried legal rule on the subject yet, and law enforcement authorities may well take the position that any gun in your house is a gun in your possession. Each family will have to weigh the benefits of keeping the spouse's and child's firearms in the house—are they for sport or self-protection, for instance—against the risk of criminal charges or having the guns forfeited.

If you have an attorney assisting you in addressing your Brady denial, be sure to raise this point in your discussions with him or her.

WHAT WILL HAPPEN TO ME?

If you get a Brady denial, don't panic. The denial may well be a mistake, and even if it's not a mistake, it may be fixable. However, successfully appealing your denial or getting the underlying disqualifying record changed will take a clear head and a calm focus through irritating paperwork and bureaucratic hoops. Angry phone calls or threats to people involved in either the underlying incident or the denial are likely to forever preclude you from getting your gun rights back. In fact, the wrong thing said in haste to the wrong person could result in you being charged with threatening a public official, assault, or disorderly conduct—none of which will help your case.

It is possible that you will be charged with a crime related to

your Brady denial. You can be charged with illegal firearms possession for guns you already own while being a prohibited person, or
you may be charged with lying on the form that you filled out at the
gun dealer for the Brady check. Again, don't panic, and don't discuss
your case with law enforcement officials, who are there to secure a
case against you for the prosecution. Exercise your right of silence
and get a criminal defense attorney as soon as possible.

In 20 years of practicing criminal defense law, I am constantly
reminded of how quickly nearly everyone forgets his right to maintain silence in a criminal investigation. I find that the nicer and more
intelligent and responsible the person who is being investigated for a
crime, the stronger his urge to just explain it all to the cops and apol-
ogize, on the theory that they can resolve it like normal human
beings instead of it turning into a cop/criminal situation.

Perhaps this is the one place where our parents screwed up. It is
ingrained in the fiber of our beings that when we break the lamp or
dent the car, we better start 'splainin'. But unless someone else might
suffer harm if you don't speak—such as you panicked and threw a gun
in the ditch by the elementary school where a child could easily pick
it up—don't talk to law enforcement until you've talked to a lawyer.

I have seen clients suffer mental breakdowns when a Brady
denial makes it necessary to reveal to family or friends a criminal
conviction or dishonorable discharge from the military from the distant past. Our vindictive, punitive society brands people who trans-
gressed the law as "criminals" or "felons," and increasingly expects
you to pay for your transgressions for the rest of your life—even if
they were the folly of youth or the desperation of hard times. It can
be extremely difficult for a person who thinks of himself as a good
American, good father, good husband, and good sportsman to realize the government views him as "a criminal." The stress of this real-
ization can wreak havoc with a person's health and well-being.

Rest assured that most good people have committed a crime at
some point in their lives. Rare is the person who never stole a piece
of candy as a child, or smashed a mailbox as a teenager, or drove
home from a wedding reception after a few beers. Nearly all of us are
"criminals" in that sense, whether or not we ever got a conviction on
our record.

Talk openly to your friends, family, clergy, or counselor, so that
you can put your Brady denial and the incident that brought it about

into perspective. Some of my clients have been able to use their Brady denial as a positive lesson to their children that the mistakes of their youth can have lasting bad consequences.

WHAT'S A FIREARM?

Brady denials affect only the possession of devices that legally qualify as firearms. Under federal law, 18 U.S.C. Section 921(3), the term "firearm" means (A) any weapon (including a starter gun) which will or is designed to or may readily be converted to expel a projectile by the action of an explosive; (B) the frame or receiver of any such weapon; (C) any firearm muffler or firearm silencer; or (D) any destructive device. Such term does not include an antique firearm.

A "destructive device" includes bombs, grenades, missiles, rockets, and similar items. An "antique firearm" includes any firearm manufactured in or before 1898, regardless of its ignition system; any replica of any pre-1898 weapon that is not designed for using rimfire or conventional centerfire fixed ammunition, or which uses ammunition not manufactured in and not commonly available in the United States; and any muzzle loading or black powder rifle, shotgun, or pistol "which cannot use fixed ammunition."

This means that under federal law, if you receive a Brady denial, you can still possess and use most black powder guns as well as archery equipment. However, some states laws are significantly more restrictive than the federal law and may prohibit you from possessing black powder as well. Comply with your state law and if your state law allows it, stick to black powder or archery while you follow the steps in this book to restore your firearms rights.

ENDNOTE

1. Fourteen states act as the full POC; another 10 are partial POC states where state agencies handle background checks or issue permits for handguns and NICS conducts the checks for long guns. Up-to-date information about the POC status of each state can be found at http://www.fbi.gov/hq/cjisd/nics.htm. Additionally, a listing of each state's published firearms, explosives, and weapons laws can be found at http://www.atf.treas.gov/pub/fire-explo_pub/states.htm.

13

2

I Didn't Know I Was Prohibited!

THE NINE FEDERAL DISQUALIFIERS

All gun owners—and particularly those who have received a Brady denial—should know and understand the list of nine disqualifying factors under the federal Gun Control Act of 1968 and its amendments. These are the nine legal reasons why a person can be prohibited from possessing firearms under federal law. The list is longer and more complicated than you might think.

The general public knows convicted felons can't have guns, but most people don't know that many misdemeanors, small property crimes, and incidents that landed you charges before you were 18 can also count as "felonies" for purpose of the federal gun laws. Despite gun control advocates screaming to the contrary, it is remarkably easy to be convicted of a felony, particularly if your conviction was 20 or 30 years ago, and not be aware that you're a convicted felon.

In addition to the "felon in possession" prohibition, there are eight other disqualifications from possessing firearms under federal law. The U.S. Supreme Court has reviewed most of these disqualifying factors and found them all constitutional. All of the federal appeals courts that have heard the issue have ruled that these firearms prohibitions do not constitute a "bill of attainder" (an unconstitutional law that punishes a particular class of people) and do not violate constitutional prohibitions against ex post facto laws (that is, even though these prohibitions are triggered by actions that may have happened long ago, this law is not considered unlawfully retroactive since it only prohibits current and future firearms possession).

Most federal appeals courts have ruled that the prohibition against possessing firearms is not punitive, saying that the federal law "is reasonably calculated to achieve a non-punitive purpose … to keep firearms out of the hands of persons who … may have a somewhat greater likelihood than other citizens to misuse firearms." *U.S. v. Munsterman*, 177 F.3d 1139 (9th Cir. 1999)(cert. den. 120 S.Ct. 279) Because the federal courts do not consider taking away your guns to be "punitive," they also don't consider it to be double jeopardy (being twice punished for the same crime).

States may have additional prohibitions, including stricter definitions of what constitutes a disqualifying criminal conviction, or requirements related to having a gun permit or license. On the other hand, your state's legal treatment of your particular case might remove it from the federal disqualification list. You will have to carefully check your state's laws as you proceed with the process of restoring your firearms rights.

There are (at the time of this writing) nine conditions under federal law that can disqualify you from lawfully possessing firearms. Under Title 18 of the United States Code, Section 922(g), it is unlawful for any person to ship, transport, possess, or receive any firearm or ammunition that has been in interstate commerce, if that person meets any of the following nine disqualifications:

1: Felony

While we commonly hear the expression "felon in possession of a firearm," the word "felony" doesn't appear in the first, and largest, federal disqualifier. The federal statute disqualifies any person "who has been convicted in any court of any crime with a potential punishment exceeding one year." 18 U.S.C. Section 922(g)(1). This means that even if you only received probation, a minor fine, a suspended sentence, or even no sentence at all, if you were convicted of a crime for which the court could legally have imposed a sentence of more than one year, the conviction *might* count as a disqualifying conviction under federal law.

Now, lawyers are fond of saying this or that *might* happen, but in this case, the vagueness is warranted. All the words in the phrase "crime with a potential punishment exceeding one year" are pretty straightforward plain English, but if you look at the statutory definitions section, you'll find it's not that simple.

Business Crime Exemptions

By definition, the term "crime punishable by imprisonment for a term exceeding one year" does not include:

> A) Any Federal or State offenses pertaining to antitrust violations, unfair trade practices, restraints of trade, or other similar offenses relating to the regulation of business practices

This means that, even if you served 15 years in jail for a white-collar business-type felony conviction, it does not prohibit you from purchasing and possessing firearms under federal law. So while stealing property worth more than $100 when you were 18 may well get you prohibited from owning guns for the rest of your life, embezzling millions as an adult may not. So if you've received a Brady denial for your felony participation in a major corporate scandal, congratulations, you get your guns back.

FELONIES AND MISDEMEANORS

A brief side trip into the history of jurisprudence will help lay the groundwork for understanding the federal firearms prohibition for misdemeanors that are treated like felonies.

In the beginning days of criminal law in the English courts, from which our own judicial system has descended, crimes weren't specifically called felonies or misdemeanors. It was just that, by definition, anything with a possible sentence of more

17

than a year was considered a felony and anything-with a possible sentence of less than a year was considered a misdemeanor. The classification of the charge was defined by the sentence.

Most actions in English courts occurred in accordance with "common law," unwritten law developed over years of practice and the accumulation of court decisions. When Americans started their own court systems, they developed a penchant for writing everything down into codes, or statutes and regulations. Those things that were felonies and those things that were misdemeanors were listed separately in these codes.

Different states and the federal government began to attach various consequences to felony convictions in addition to the actual sentence. In many states, people lose the right to vote or to serve on juries, at least temporarily, when convicted of a felony. The federal government today attaches numerous punishments to having a felony conviction, in addition to the firearms prohibition. People who have had a felony conviction cannot get many student loans, government-backed mortgages and business start-up grants, and cannot work in federal buildings or receive government contracts. Many foreign countries won't give you a travel visa if you have a felony conviction, and others, like Canada, won't let you in unless you pay a large amount of money for the privilege. It's often said, not without some merit, that the only thing you can do once you have a felony conviction is make your living by crime.

Certain State Misdemeanors

The second exemption is where many folks, even lawyers who ought to know better, start to get baffled. Paragraph B exempts:

> B) Any State offense classified by the laws of the State as a misdemeanor and punishable by a term of imprisonment of two years or less. 18 U.S.C. Section 921(a)(20).

Over the years, many states decided to get tough on various violations of the law such as driving while intoxicated, yet did not want to attach the full weight of a felony conviction to these offenses. The sentences for first or second DWIs and other criminal offenses in many states increased beyond one year, but the state continued to call the convictions "misdemeanors" so that people convicted of them did not lose the rights of citizenship or economic privileges that they would with something called a "felony."

Under the federal definitions, conviction for a state crime that is called a misdemeanor does not disqualify you from firearms possession under federal law if the state misdemeanor has a maximum potential sentence of two years or less. If the state misdemeanor has a maximum potential sentence of two years and one day or more, you are prohibited from possessing firearms under federal law.

This means a misdemeanor DWI conviction from a state like Vermont, which has sentences of less than two years for DWI #1 misdemeanors, may mean you can have guns, while a misdemeanor DWI conviction from another state like Massachusetts, which has three-year sentences for DWI #1 misdemeanors, means you are prohibited from having guns—even if the facts of the case underlying the conviction were exactly the same in both states.

No one said it was going to be logical.

What Constitutes a Conviction?

The definition of what constitutes a "crime punishable by imprisonment for a term exceeding one year" does not stop there. It goes on to state as follows:

19

> What constitutes a conviction of such a crime
> shall be determined in accordance with the law of
> the jurisdiction in which the proceedings were held.

Whether or not someone has been convicted of a crime is not always cut-and-dried. Many states have procedures by which a charge is filed or deferred, with the intention being that if the person charged doesn't get into trouble during some intervening period of time, the charge will be dismissed or a not-guilty judgment entered. Some states simply leave these charges open indefinitely, and if the person ever picks up another criminal charge, the prior open charge is resurrected and acted on. Whether for purposes of a firearms purchase or for federal crimes sentencing or for any other reason where a person's criminal history has to be assessed, it is often extremely difficult to determine whether something should be considered a "conviction." The statutes or regulations of the state where the conviction happened might help in this process, but often as not, the marking of convictions as filed or open is a matter of common-law court practice that cannot be explained with any degree of certainty.

Finally, the definition of the so-called felony disqualification says,

> Any conviction which has been expunged, or set
> aside, or for which a person has been pardoned or
> has had civil rights restored shall not be considered
> a conviction for purposes of this chapter, unless
> such pardon, expungement, or restoration of civil
> rights expressly provides that the person may not
> ship, transport, possess, or receive firearms.
> 18 U.S.C. Section 921(a)(20).

The ATF has seen fit to add another proviso to the definition that Congress has devised in the statute, adding "or unless the person is prohibited by the law of the jurisdiction in which the proceedings were held from receiving or possessing any firearms." 27 CFR Section 478.11. There do not appear to be any federal court decisions yet that would determine whether ATF's addition to the statutory definition is lawful.

Expungements and pardons are two of the ways that are discussed later in this book for removing a criminal conviction from your record. Setting aside a conviction is usually related to the resolution of filed or deferred charges. The question of restoration of civil rights, however, is more complex.

Restoration of Civil Rights

In many states, if you are convicted of a felony or even some misdemeanors, you lose certain of your civil rights, including the right to vote, to serve in office, or to sit on a jury. If you lose one or more of these rights by virtue of a conviction and *then get these rights back*, either automatically at the end of a term of probation and parole or after a certain period of time, or by some application procedure, your conviction no longer counts under federal law to preclude you from firearms possession. In other words, if you are convicted of armed robbery in a state that prohibits you from voting until you are satisfactorily discharged from parole, and you are discharged from parole and get your voting rights back, you are also permitted by federal law to purchase and possess firearms.

However, some states do not take away these fundamental rights of citizenship when a person is convicted of a crime. If you are convicted of a felony property crime (like our example of stealing property worth more than $100 when you were 18) in a state like Vermont, which never takes away any of your rights of citizenship due to a conviction, you can never get those rights reinstated, and thus even long after you're released from parole or probation you are prohibited by federal law from possessing a firearm.

This prohibition also applies if you are "under indictment" or otherwise currently charged with a crime that might be punishable by a year or more in jail.

And the gun control folks wonder how it is that someone can be convicted of a felony and not know it.

2: Fugitive from Justice

The second disqualification from firearms possession under federal law is anyone "who is a fugitive from justice." 18 U.S.C. Section 922(g)(2).

The gun control law defines "fugitive from justice" as "any person who has fled from any State to avoid prosecution for a crime or to avoid giving testimony in any criminal proceeding." 18 U.S.C. Section 921(a)(15). The ATF regulations expand this, adding, "This term also includes any person who knows that misdemeanor or felony charges are pending against such person and who leaves the State of prosecution." 27 CFR Section 478.11. There is no case law on the books yet to determine whether this agency expansion of the definition is lawful.

It is generally accepted that "fugitive from justice" means someone for whom there is a pending arrest warrant. Warrants can be issued whenever someone does not come into court when required, including your failure to pay a speeding ticket that you got while on vacation in a distant state. But under the statute, you do not even need to be the person charged with a crime to be a "fugitive from justice." If you are scheduled to be a witness in a criminal proceeding and leave the state, you can also be considered a fugitive from justice. Neither the statute nor the ATF regulations are clear as to whether this only applies when you've received a witness subpoena, or at what point in someone else's criminal process this requirement that you not leave the state attaches.

The expanded ATF definition also leaves open the question of whether someone who leaves the state in which they are being prosecuted with that court's permission could be charged for firearms violations. Most people who are charged with a misdemeanor are not held in jail pending the outcome of their case. A pending misdemeanor charge would not otherwise preclude anyone from possessing a firearm. And most defendants in misdemeanor cases are not required by the court to remain in the state. Under a literal reading of the ATF regulation, if a person who received a citation to appear in court in three months' time for a misdemeanor trespass charge for participating in a political protest decides to drive to another state to deer hunt, that person can be charged as a federal fugitive from justice in possession of a firearm.

If there is a warrant out for your arrest, you will receive a Brady denial until your warrant is cleared. If your warrant is for something like a speeding ticket, it is not likely that police will arrive at your door to arrest you; but if your warrant is for anything more serious, once your name appears in the NICS computer as being at a certain location, attached to a certain address, you are likely to be arrested shortly unless you can clear up the warrant.

3: Drug User or Addict

Federal law prohibits firearm possession by any person "who is an unlawful user of or addicted to any controlled substance." 18 U.S.C. Section 922(g)(3). The federal statute does not include a definition for this section, but the ATF regulations make it clear that a conviction for drug use or possession is *not necessary* to be disqualified under this section of the federal law:

"A person who uses a controlled substance and has lost the power of self-control with reference to the use of controlled substance; and any person who is a current user of a controlled substance in a manner other than as prescribed by a licensed physician. Such use is not limited to the use of drugs on a particular day, or within a matter or days or weeks before, but rather that the unlawful use has occurred recently enough to indicate that the individual is actively engaged in such conduct. A person may be an unlawful current user of a controlled substance even though the substance is not being used at the precise time the person seeks to acquire a firearm or receives or possesses a firearm. An inference of current use may be drawn from evidence of a recent use or possession of a controlled substance or a pattern of use or possession that reasonably covers the present time, e.g. a conviction for use or possession of a controlled substance within the past year; multiple arrests for such offenses within the past five years if the most recent arrest occurred within the past year; or persons found through a drug test to use a controlled substance unlawfully, provided that the test was administered within the past year. For a current or former member of the Armed Forces, an inference of current use may be drawn from recent disciplinary or other administrative action based on confirmed drug use, e.g. court martial conviction, nonjudicial punishment, or an administrative discharge based on drug use or drug rehabilitation failure." 27 CFR Section 478.11.

This prohibition may be the most troubling of all nine, in that it requires no conviction or court action whatsoever to render a person

23

disqualified. Although the ATF regulation goes to some lengths to say that criminal convictions (including misdemeanors) for drug possession can be evidence that someone is a prohibited "known drug user," it is also clear that mere arrests—with no convictions resulting—will also result in a firearms prohibition. The regulation also leaves open the fact that this prohibition can be based on any number of other sources of information.

One source of this information can be your criminal record—even if you have no history of arrests—and a related database used by police called the Spillman Names Table. Law enforcement officials can put considerably more information into your criminal record than simply your arrests and convictions. State and federal criminal records include places to enter descriptors including physical appearance, tattoos, or recognizable characteristics. They can also enter statements about a person's character or behavior, including things like "known gang member" or "known cocaine user."

When Brady background checks began, but before the NICS system went into effect, the chief local law enforcement official of the town where the person applying for a gun lived gave the Brady approval or denial. Under that system (known as CLEO for "chief law enforcement officer"), many people received denials when their local police chief deemed them drug users. This disqualification was fertile grounds for abuse, as small-town police chiefs entered Brady denials for long-haired, Harley-riding citizens or others who irked them by simply stating the applicant was a "pot smoker" or user of other controlled substances. People denied under such circumstances had virtually no recourse other than to move away—which was probably the police chief's hope in the first place.

Today, fewer denials seem to be based on this particular disqualification, but those who are denied on these grounds still have little recourse. It is extremely difficult to prove a negative—that is, to prove that you aren't a user of controlled substances. This is one of the more frustrating denials to try to overturn, as well as one that seems highly offensive to our standards of justice and innocence until proven guilty.

The armed forces Veterans Administration recently uploaded nearly 100,000 mental health records of veterans into the NICS database. Many veterans who received medical discharges from the military did so on the grounds of mental health issues that were determined in military judicial or administrative hearings; some of these no doubt mentioned drug use, and we are likely to see these records be used as grounds for Brady denials to these mostly Vietnam-era veterans.

4: Mental Defect

Federal law prohibits firearms possession by any person "who has been adjudicated as a mental defective or who has been committed to a mental institution." 18 U.S.C. Section 922(g)(4). Like the prohibition against gun ownership by persons who are known drug users, this disqualifier relies heavily on the personal knowledge of law enforcement officials. It also presents a conundrum: Since health records generally, and mental health records in particular, are subject to strict legal privacy requirements, how would such information get into the NICS databases?

The answer lies in part on the grounds that this prohibition hinges on the adjudication of mental defect in a court or a court's action in committing a person to a mental institution. The ATF regulations define "adjudicated as a mental defective" as:

(a) a determination by a court, board, commission, or other lawful authority that a person, as a result of marked subnormal intelligence, or mental illness, incompetency, condition, or disease: (1) is a danger to himself or to others; or, (2) lacks the mental capacity to contract or manage his own affairs. (b) The term shall include (1) a finding of insanity by a court in a criminal case; and (2) those persons found incompetent to stand trial or found not guilty by reason of lack of mental responsibility pursuant to articles 50a and 72b of the Uniform Code of Military Justice, 10 U.S.C. Sections 850a, 876b. 27 CFR Section 478.11.

The ATF regulations define "committed to a mental institution" to mean a formal commitment of a person to a mental institution by a court, board, commission, or other lawful authority. The term includes a commitment to a mental institution involuntarily. The term includes commitment for mental defectiveness or mental illness. It also includes commitments for other reasons, such as for drug use. The term does not include a person in a mental institution for observation or a voluntary admission to a mental institution. 27 CFR Section 478.11.

Of the nearly 100,000 mental health records of veterans that were recently uploaded into the NICS database, many refer to mental health related medical discharges from the military. It appears that NICS and ATF are now considering this to be an adjudication of mental defect under the gun control statute, which would seem to be effectively a new regulation or a new interpretation of the statute without going through the public due process of adopting a new regulation, but this issue has yet to be addressed in federal court.

At the time of this writing, the president had just announced his intention to create a national database of health treatment records, which no doubt will be accessible to NICS, resulting in more disqualifications under this section.[1]

5. Illegal Aliens

The fifth disqualifier for firearms possession is any person who, "being an alien, is illegally or unlawfully in the United States; or, … has been admitted to the United States under a non-immigrant visa." 18 U.S.C. Section 922(g)(5). There are exceptions for foreign diplomats and other members of foreign governments, as well as for people coming to the United States for lawful hunting or sporting events who have the proper permits and licenses for them.

6. Dishonorable Discharge

The federal firearms prohibition attaches to anyone "who has been discharged from the Armed Forces under dishonorable conditions." 18 U.S.C. Section 922(g)(6). There are numerous levels of discharge from the Armed Services, many of which are other than honorable. Only the lowest level, actual dishonorable discharge, triggers the federal firearm prohibition.

7. Renounced U.S. Citizenship

The seventh federal firearms disqualifier applies to anyone

"who, having been a citizen of the United States, has renounced his citizenship." 18 U.S. C. Section 922(g)(7). While the federal statute does not define what is meant by renouncing one's citizenship, ATF regulations state, "A person has renounced his U.S. citizenship if the person, having been a citizen of the United States, has renounced citizenship either (1) before a diplomatic or consular officer of the United States in a foreign state … or (2) before an officer designated by the Attorney General when the United States is in a state of war…." 27 CFR Section 478.11

This seems to be the federal firearms prohibition category applied least often. The renunciation of U.S. citizenship referred to means formal renunciation related with becoming a citizen of another country or joining an enemy military force. The ATF regulation on this point makes it clear that this prohibition is not to be applied to drunken declarations made in disgust at presidential election results or the final score of the Army-Navy football game.

8. Domestic Abuse Prevention Order

The final two federal firearms disqualifications relate to domestic violence. Number eight precludes firearms possession by anyone who is subject to a family court abuse prevention order or domestic restraining order that:

> A) was issued after a hearing of which such person received actual notice and at which such person had an opportunity to participate;
>
> B) restrains such person from harassing, stalking, or threatening an intimate partner of such person or child of such intimate partner or person, or engaging in other conduct that would place an intimate partner in reasonable fear of bodily injury to the partner or child; and,
>
> C) i. Includes a finding that such person represents a credible threat to the physical safety of such intimate partner or child, or
>
> ii. By its terms explicitly prohibits the use, attempted use, or threatened use of physical force

against such intimate partner or child that would reasonably be expected to cause bodily injury. 18 U.S.C. Section 922(g)(8).

An "intimate partner" for purposes of this statute is defined as "the spouse of the person, a former spouse of the person, an individual who is a parent of a child with the person, and an individual who cohabitates or has cohabitated with the person." 18 U.S.C. Section 921. Thus a stay-away order from someone who the person was merely dating, or any other kind of no-trespass order such as from a workplace or school, would not disqualify you from possessing firearms.

9. Misdemeanor Crime of Domestic Violence

The last current firearms prohibition factor is for any person "who has been convicted in a court of a misdemeanor crime of domestic violence." 18 U.S.C. Section 922(g)(9). This is the most recently added federal disqualifier, and possibly the most controversial. It is certainly the most confusing, starting with being defined as "Except as provided in subparagraph C" when there *is* no subparagraph C. 18 U.S.C. Section 921(a)(33).

The missing subparagraph C aside, "the term 'misdemeanor crime of domestic violence' means an offense that (i) is a misdemeanor under Federal or State law; and (ii) has, as an element, the use or attempted use of physical force, or the threatened use of a deadly weapon, committed by a current or former spouse, parent, or guardian of the victim, by a person with whom the victim shares a child in common, by a person who is cohabitating with or has cohabitated with the victim as a spouse, parent, or guardian, or by a person similarly situated to a spouse, parent, or guardian of the victim."

Thus the misdemeanor crime of domestic violence section of the gun control law has a broader definition of a domestic partner than does the preceding section related to stay-away orders involving an "intimate partner." A stay-away order from one's parent or guardian would not trigger a firearms prohibition number eight; a conviction for misdemeanor assault on one's parent or guardian would trigger the firearms prohibition number nine. ATF regulations on this point track the statutory language, adding small bits of explanation but not altering the definitions.

The more confusing aspect of this prohibition is that it does not matter what the misdemeanor conviction is called under state law, as long as the facts underlying the conviction involve the use or attempted use of force or the threatened use of a deadly weapon, and someone who qualifies as a domestic partner. This means that convictions for disorderly conduct or simple assault, if they involve, say, shoving the person you live with, or even publicly spanking a child, would count under the federal gun control statute to prohibit you from firearms possession. The statute that you are convicted under does not need to contain reference to a domestic relationship for the conviction to disqualify you under the gun control statutes; *if the underlying facts involved a domestic partner and physical force, the conviction counts, no matter what it is called.*

On the other hand, ironically, it is not inconceivable that there are convictions for misdemeanors that are called "domestic assaults" that *do not* trigger the federal firearms prohibition. In many states, the criminal definition of "assault" can involve intimidation or making the victim afraid but not necessarily involve physical force or the threat of a deadly weapon. Many people across the country have been convicted of something called "domestic assault" for telling their soon-to-be-ex-spouse that if they don't stop yelling, they will go jump off a bridge, or will call the social service agency to take away the children, or will tell their boss that they do drugs. None of these situations involve physical force or threatened use of a deadly weapon, and even though they are called "domestic assault," should not prohibit someone from possessing firearms.

However, misdemeanor domestic violence firearms prohibitions are just beginning to come through the federal courts, and it is too soon to determine where the federal courts will draw the line as to what meets the federal firearms prohibition and what doesn't.

The statute and ATF regulations make clear that in states that don't classify crimes as felonies and misdemeanors, this prohibition applies to all convictions with a potential sentence of one year or less, including magistrate-court type cases that resulted in fines only. Many states, such as South Carolina, previously treated misdemeanor domestic cases as tickets—similarly to fish and game or traffic tickets. The citation was to a magistrate court, a small fine was paid, and the person charged went on his way. This treatment was used as a law enforcement tool to break up relatively minor family arguments that required some helpful intervention to let tempers cool but did not warrant criminal court charges. Unfortunately, such minor proceedings from the past now count to prohibit the people involved—who had no reason at the time to consider the situation anything other than a minor embarrassment and inconvenience—from exercising their constitutional firearms rights.

Because the misdemeanor domestic violence disqualification is still relatively new, many people remain confused as to the fact that it is applied retroactively. No matter how long ago your domestic violence conviction occurred, if the conviction meets the standards for this disqualification, you are prohibited from possessing firearms. Like the felon-in-possession law, this prohibition has been challenged in federal court and found to be legal, even when your conviction was decades ago and you were never told—in fact, couldn't have been told, because nobody knew—that it would have the effect of depriving you of your firearms on some future date.

The misdemeanor domestic violence prohibition does include a list of protective criteria that must be met in order for the conviction to count. For example, to count as a conviction, the person must have either been tried by a jury or knowingly and intelligently waived his right to jury trial; and have been represented by an attorney, or knowingly and intelligently waived his right to counsel. As with felony convictions, a misdemeanor crime of domestic violence doesn't "count" if the conviction has been expunged or set aside, or if the person convicted had certain civil rights removed and then restored.

Unlike the felony disqualifier, neither the statute nor the ATF regulations say that you are disqualified during the time that you are charged, but not yet convicted, of a misdemeanor crime of domestic violence. As a practical matter, in most cases where there is a charge of a misdemeanor crime of domestic violence, there will be an open domestic restraining order that works as a separate disqualifier. In many other cases the charges are originally brought as felonies, in which case the felony indictment disqualifier applies. However, if

30

you have received a Brady denial for a pending misdemeanor domestic charge and there is not a restraining order against you, you should certainly make the argument in administrative appeal that the prohibition does not apply.

ADDITIONAL STATE LAW DISQUALIFIERS

States may impose additional firearms disqualifications that are more stringent than the federal law. State laws commonly preclude from firearms possession anyone who is on probation or parole, even for a crime that does not qualify as a federal "felony" or "domestic violence misdemeanor." States that require firearms permits have disqualifiers for people who do not have a permit or have had their permit revoked. Some states list additional disqualifying misdemeanors, such as drug or violence convictions. You will have to check your state statutes carefully or review your state disqualifiers with an attorney licensed in your state to be certain you understand your state's firearms disqualifications.

ENDNOTE

1. Concern over the privacy of mental health records relative to firearms transactions has raised the interest of some civil liberties groups who have not previously taken an active interest in private firearms ownership. See, for example, the Web site of the Electronic Privacy Information Center at http://www.epic.org/privacy/firearms regarding gun owners' privacy.

3

Checks, Appeals, and the Myth about ATF

THE BRADY CHECK

Every person who seeks to purchase a firearm—long gun or handgun—from an FFL must submit to a Brady background check. This is because FFLs are not allowed to sell a firearm to a person unless they have been told they may proceed, or unless after properly submitting the request, three business days have elapsed and the FFL has gotten no answer from the NICS system. Brady checks are not currently required for sales of firearms by individuals who are not FFLs, such as a person who is simply selling off his own personal firearm. Brady checks are also not required for persons carrying a firearms license in states that have qualifying licensing programs.

Brady checks can only legally be done by an FFL "in connection with a proposed firearm transfer as required by the Brady act. FFLs are strictly prohibited from initiating a NICS background check for any other purpose." 28 CFR Section 25.6. This strict prohibition is meant to keep Brady checks limited to the purpose of firearms purchases and prevent FFLs from entering into a sideline business of selling criminal background checks for employers or other investigations. Despite the clear restrictions of this language, at least one national retail store that has a firearms department is known for conducting Brady checks for the purchase of black powder guns that are not "firearms" within the definition of the federal gun control statute; however, to date no one has challenged this in court, so there has not been a ruling as to whether this is legal.

To start the Brady check process, the person who wishes to purchase a firearm must complete ATF Form 4473. This form asks questions about the purchaser's identity and criminal history and other information relative to the firearms statutes. The form also requests the purchaser's Social Security number. Technically speaking, this entry is optional; however, in my experience, every time anyone I know has tried to purchase a firearm without submitting a Social Security number, a delay has resulted. The fact that the Social Security number is shared with any number of FFL employees and worse, that it is read out loud during the FFL's phone call to NICS for the Brady check, would seem to be an unlawful violation of the privacy protections that are supposed to be attached to a Social Security number—but given that Social Security numbers are now used for everything from health insurance to fishing licenses, I don't suppose this practice will stop anytime soon.

It is *very important* that you read Form 4473 carefully, including reading the instructional material and definitions on the back of the form. If you are in doubt as to whether a past criminal conviction might disqualify you, it would be smart to check with an attorney before filling it out. You must sign Form 4473, swearing that the information you have completed on it is true and correct to the best of your knowledge. Providing false information on this form is considered perjury, and many people get criminally charged for providing inaccurate information.

In addition to filling out the 4473, the firearms purchaser must provide proof of identification. Proper photo identification must be provided, and if there is a question about the identification, the FFL is authorized to request better identification or to tell NICS that the identification is inadequate.

Once the form is filled out and identification documents provided, the FFL will telephone either one of two FBI NICS system calling centers, or a state POC. The FFL will read the information provided on the form, as well as information from the identifying documentation, to the NICS or POC personnel over the phone. There is no requirement that this be conducted in private, and in most gun shops it's done right at the counter.

The FFL will also tell the NICS or POC person what kind of firearm(s) you are attempting to purchase. The agencies claim that this information is not unlawful firearm registration but rather is necessary to processing the Brady check because, for example, there are different age requirements for the purchase of a handgun or a long gun.

With this information, the NICS personnel or the state POC will search three major databases: NCIC, III, and the NICS Index (state POCs may also have access to additional state data). The NCIC (National Crime Information Center) is a database of more than 750,000 records regarding warrants, fugitives from justice, and disqualifying restraining orders. The III (Interstate Identification Index or "Triple I") contains more than 35 million criminal records and is cross-referenced to the FBI's Automated Fingerprint Identification System (AFIS), which is why Brady appeals must include fingerprints. The NICS Index is a special FBI database containing information from federal and state agencies about people who are prohibited from having firearms for reasons other than being a fugitive from justice, having a disqualifying restraining order against them, or having a disqualifying criminal conviction. This information may include records regarding illegal aliens; records regarding persons who local police consider to be "known drug users" even though they don't have criminal convictions; and mental health records indicating that a person is prohibited from having a firearm due to mental defect. In other words, the NICS Index contains a list of people for whom various state and federal agencies have jotted a note saying, "Don't sell this person a gun."

Within a short period of time—typically a few minutes to a half hour depending on the time, day, and season of the call—NICS or the POC will give the FFL one of three responses: denied, delayed, or proceed. If the FFL receives a "proceed," he may go ahead and lawfully sell you the firearm, unless the FFL has additional information leading him to believe that it would be unlawful for you to possess a firearm. In other words, even if the NICS or POC gives the transaction a "proceed," the FFL can still refuse to sell you the firearm if he believes it would be illegal. For example, the FFL may be aware that you have a criminal conviction that, for some reason, hasn't shown up in the computer system. Or the FFL may have reason to believe you are a known drug user or were committed to a mental institution. In such cases, the FFL can refuse to sell you the firearm.

If the FFL receives a "delayed" response, it means that NICS or the POC needs more time to process the request. It is important not to panic if you receive a delay on a Brady check. The FFL standing there with the phone in his hand has no idea whatsoever why there is a delay, so there is no point in yelling at him. The FFL is usually highly motivated to sell you the firearm, since that's how he makes his living, so he is usually as upset as you are by a delay.

A delay often has nothing whatsoever to do with you or your circumstances. It can occur because you've happened to call at a busy time (like the Saturday before deer season, or during the winter weekend of a large gun show), because there is a computer systems problem at NICS, because NICS or the POC are shorthanded because of a flu epidemic, or any number of other reasons unrelated to you and your purchase.

If you receive a delay, it is important to not start talking about it or guessing the reasons why you might be delayed. Remember, the FFL has the ability to deny you the purchase even if you get a Brady check approval. If you stand at the counter nervously rattling off the list of your youthful indiscretions that you think might be holding up the process, you may be handing the FFL reason to deny you.

If your attempt to purchase a firearm has met with a Brady check delay, NICS or the POC has three business days to get back to the FFL with either a "proceed" or a denial. If NICS or the POC does not get back to the FFL by the fourth business day, he or she is free to lawfully sell you the gun.

DENIED: WHAT TO DO FIRST

If the FFL calling in your Brady check is told that you have been denied, the FFL will give you a NICS Transaction Number (NTN) to identify your attempted firearms transaction. The FFL is also supposed to give you a brochure that has been prepared by the FBI's

NICS division regarding your rights and responsibilities after a Brady denial. If your state uses a POC, the POC may have prepared its own appeals brochure in addition to the NICS brochure.

The first step you should take if you receive a Brady denial is to make sure that you get your NTN from the FFL. If your FFL has the FBI's brochure, make sure you also get that. It has a space on the front for the FFL to write your NTN on it so that you don't lose it. While most people are angry, embarrassed, or confused at the moment they get a Brady denial, it is again important that you not discuss it. You may think that you know why you received the denial, but you may well be wrong.

As soon as you can access a typewriter or computer, you should write a letter requesting the statement of reasons for your denial from the denying agency. Your FFL should provide you with the name and mailing address of the agency that issued the denial. In most states, it will be the FBI's NICS department, but in some states it will be the state agency that is designated the Brady check POC.

In almost every jurisdiction, you must make this request in writing. Some states that have POCs allow you to request the statement of reasons by phone or in person; however, since you may well be appealing the decision, it is better to have a record of your request in writing anyway. It also helps you avoid getting into an argument with someone on the phone or in person.

The letter to either NICS or your state POC agency must include your complete mailing address as well as the NTN.

If you want to, you can also submit a set of your fingerprints with this initial request for the statement of reasons for the denial. While it isn't required at this stage, if your denial was based on a simple mistake of identity, including your fingerprints could well resolve the matter without needing to proceed to a formal appeals process.

You can get your fingerprints rolled at a local law enforcement agency, usually a sheriff's or constable's office. The "10 card" of your rolled fingerprints must be noted "for NICS purposes only." The law enforcement agency is entitled to charge you for the fingerprint service, and you may need to make an appointment some days or weeks in advance depending on how busy the law enforcement agency is. I again urge you to restrain yourself from talking about the reasons you think you might have gotten a Brady denial while you are getting your fingerprints done. You are under no obligation to give law enforcement officers any more information about yourself than is necessary, and although it may be tempting to engage in a sociable conversation with the sheriff's deputy who is taking your fingerprints just for politeness' sake, keep that conversation to topics like sports and the weather rather than your criminal history or Brady status.

A sample Request for Reasons for Denial letter is found at the end of this book. Be sure to make a copy of your letter before you send it and a copy of your fingerprint card if you are sending one. This is a good time to start a file for this information; keep it in a safe place where it is unlikely to get lost or shuffled in with other paperwork. Also, carefully check your letter before you send it and have someone else proofread it for you—it must have your accurate street address and the correct NTN number.

The NICS Appeals Services Team (AST) will respond to your request for the reasons for your denial within five business days after receipt of your letter. You will receive a statement of reasons in writing. If the denial is related to your criminal history, you will usually receive a copy of the criminal record indicating the date, conviction, and the charging agency (that is, which police department or other office charged you with the crime).

THE ADMINISTRATIVE BRADY APPEAL

Once you receive the statement explaining the reason for your Brady denial, you will have to decide whether to appeal. There will be instructions in the statement telling you what information to send if you do wish to appeal your denial. There is some cost involved in appealing your Brady denial to NICS—an administrative appeal fee, the fee for having your fingerprints done, and copying costs for the copies of the criminal conviction or other material related to your appeal. Still, compared to the loss of your ability to exercise your firearms rights, the price of an administrative appeal is relatively small. If you received your Brady denial in a POC state, you may choose to appeal either to the state agency that issued the denial or directly to NICS. If your appeal to the state agency upholds the denial, you can still appeal to NICS after that, giving you two bites at the apple. If the reason for your denial involved one of your own state's records, then an appeal within your state, where the state agency is more familiar with the records, may give you a better chance of overturning the denial than proceeding to NICS. But if your denial involved an out-of-state or federal record, you might want to skip the state agency appeal and proceed directly to the NICS appeals process, where the people handling the appeal will have greater familiarity with other states' records.

Some people feel that they would rather not appeal their Brady denial, out of fear that it is calling more attention to themselves; no one wants to unnecessarily raise a red flag in a law enforcement computer program. As a result, many people who are legally entitled to possess firearms live quietly with a Brady denial because of fear of pursuing a just, legal resolution with their government. This is what civil liberties lawyers call a "chilling effect," and it is one of the main ways that our rights as citizens get eroded year after year. Still, each individual must make this decision for himself, balancing his personal life, his family, and his economic circumstances with the issues at stake.

As the NICS system and law enforcement agencies get more efficient regarding issues of firearms law enforcement, however, it's not the filing of a Brady appeal that will trigger unwanted police attention, but the initial Brady denial itself. Brady denials are reported directly to the U.S. Attorney's office and the ATF office for the jurisdiction that you live in; as money for federal law enforcement increases, with more federal officers in the field due to increasing security funding, and as more state and local law enforcement officers are trained to cooperate with federal agencies on firearms matters, Brady denials become more likely to trigger immediate police action, whether or not you decide to appeal the denial. This being the case, we are likely to see the "chilling effect" occurring not at the point of a Brady denial appeal, but rather at the initial decision to buy a firearm from an FFL. Once you've made that decision and received a denial, filing an appeal will not likely make the circumstances any worse.

39

Another factor to consider in deciding whether to file a Brady administrative appeal is whether your case is the type that will require going back into the original court to correct a record first. If, for example, your criminal record shows that you have an open, pending case or a warrant out for you, but actually the case was closed long ago and the warrant removed, you will have to go back to the original court and make sure that they correct the record before the NICS AST can overturn your Brady denial. In such a case you may want to consider getting the record corrected before proceeding with your appeal. The information in the chapters that follow regarding specific techniques for approaching denials for each of the different prohibiting factors can help you to make this decision.

If you file an appeal, you must include your fingerprint card if you have not already done so. Additionally, you should state the reasons for your appeal (for technical reasons that may help if your appeal has to go any further, I'd suggest you include language that says you are appealing "for reasons that include the following" so as not to preclude other options you don't currently know about—see the sample appeal letter at the end of this book) and attach copies of any relevant records that support your argument that your denial should be overturned.

It is probably helpful to have an attorney assist you in drafting your Brady appeal. It is very easy to get off track as to the issues that are relevant on your appeal, or to volunteer too much information on points that won't make a difference in your appeal but could wind up generating other problems. Additionally, there may be more reasons for your appeal to be overturned than you've thought about—just like having your taxes done by a professional often reveals more deductions than you knew you could use.

Even if the denying agency was a state POC, you may choose to file your appeal either with the state or with the NICS AST. Consider whether you think your state agency or NICS would do a better job of understanding the records that are causing a problem, if you know what they are. If you've got a sharp, trustworthy person in charge of your state POC or criminal records system, you may feel more comfortable dealing with them regarding your Brady denial. If you don't think your state agency personnel may be up to interpreting an old, confusing, out-of-state criminal record, you may be better off going to the NICS AST.

Within a reasonable period of time, you will receive a written decision from NICS AST on your appeal. If your appeal is successful, you will be notified that your denial has been overturned. You must present the letter from NICS AST to your FFL when you go to buy the firearm. If it is within 30 days of the initial denial, NICS will issue a "proceed" to the FFL and you can go ahead and purchase your firearm without going through the process again. However, if your appeal involved obtaining your old criminal records or you've hired a lawyer to assist you, it's unlikely that you'll be receiving your response from your appeal within 30 days of the initial denial. In that case, you'll have to reinitiate the purchase by filling out a new Form 4473.

APPEAL TO FEDERAL COURT

If your Brady denial appeal to NICS is unsuccessful, you still have a number of options available to you. The top two options are either to attack the disqualification back in the original jurisdiction—discussed in the chapters that follow—or file a lawsuit in federal court seeking to have your denial overturned or the record corrected.

By FBI regulation, "an individual may also contest the accuracy or validity of a disqualifying record by bringing an action against the state or political subdivision responsible for providing the contested information, or responsible for denying the transfer, or against the United States, as the case may be, for an order directing that the contested information be corrected or that the firearm transfer be approved." 28 CFR Section 25.11.

"Bringing an action" in this case means filing a lawsuit. Although some people represent themselves in federal court, if you are bringing a lawsuit against the United States Department of Justice or against a state, it is wise to be represented by an attorney. Federal lawsuits, especially against state or federal agencies, involve very specific procedures and filing requirements. If you proceed on your own, without an attorney's advice, you may well wind up having your suit dismissed because of errors in filing or

41

service requirements before you have opportunity for a hearing on the merits of your case.

Unfortunately, because filing a lawsuit to correct an erroneous Brady denial is not a criminal case, you cannot get assigned a public defender to represent you; you must hire a lawyer privately. This can be quite expensive. I am not aware of any nonprofit organizations or firearms owners groups at this time who are helping firearms owners with the legal fees for appealing Brady denials. Most firearms owners groups have expressed that they want to stay far away from the politically and emotionally charged issue of "letting criminals have guns." Given the number of erroneous denials or technically correct denials that are for stupid, inappropriate reasons, it is a shame that some of these talk-tough groups have not become active in restoring firearms rights.

In addition to the cost of paying an attorney to file a federal lawsuit, there will be other out-of-pocket costs, including a filing fee and service of process fees totaling several hundred dollars, possibly charges for copying, obtaining certified records, witness fees and travel expenses for ordinary factual witnesses whom you subpoena, and any expert witness fees. There is also the time involved, because even when you have a lawyer, being the party to a federal lawsuit involves considerable participation on your part. Ultimately it will involve attending court hearings, testifying, and being cross-examined, which often involves being asked accusatory questions that are quite upsetting, possibly even humiliating.

At the end of that process, if you prevail, your Brady denial will be overturned. However, the statute contains no provisions for receiving any damages or even repayment of your attorney's fees, although under the civil practice rules in federal court, that may be a possibility.

All that aside, there are times when filing suit in federal court is the only option to resolve your Brady denial (other than the continuing option to simply live with the denial and divest yourself of your firearms forever). Whoever said "freedom isn't free" probably wasn't thinking about how much money people have to shell out to get their Brady denials overturned in federal court, but it makes just as much sense here. Citizens often have to fight hard to maintain the rights that ought to be theirs by law, and bringing suit to restore your Second Amendment rights may just be one such place where fighting hard is necessary. As we said before, each individual firearms owner will have to decide whether filing a federal lawsuit to restore his firearms rights is the right thing to do, balancing his finances, personal position, and family considerations.

THE MYTH OF THE ATF REMOVAL OF DISABILITIES PROCESS

On paper, there is a legal process that a firearms owner who has received a Brady denial can go through to apply to ATF to be "relieved from disabilities" under the gun control statutes. According to ATF regulations, 27 CFR Section 478.144, "any person may make application for relief from the disabilities under section 922(g) and (n) of the Act." The regulation goes on to describe in detail the method for applying to the ATF, including filing an application form, three letters of reference, copies of the court record that disqualified the person from firearms possession, and consent to allow ATF to investigate.

This regulation says that after investigation the ATF "may grant relief to an applicant if it is established ... that the circumstances regarding the disability, and the applicant's record and reputation, are such that the applicant will not be likely to act in a manner dangerous to public safety, and that the granting of the relief would not be contrary to the public interest." 27 CFR Section 478.144(d). While the regulation states that the agency will not grant relief until at least two years after a person has been released from probation or parole, the agency previously required the passage of 10 years before it would consider such applications.

The unfortunate thing here is the word "previously." While this provision remains as a lawful regulation on the books, Congress has precluded ATF from processing these restoration applications since 1994 by specifically declining to fund them.

Several gun owners since 1994 have challenged the ATF's refusal to process restoration applications, but the federal courts have turned down each of the challenges, noting that Congress has the power to amend or even effectively repeal a statute by an appropriations bill, as long as it is clear about what it has done. The House Appropriations Committee in its report on the fiscal year 1994 budget stated that an ATF determination as to whether someone is still a danger to public safety "is a very difficult and subjective task which could have devastating consequences for innocent citizens if the wrong decision is made." The committee went on to say that the resources spent processing firearms rights restoration applications would be better spent fighting violent crimes—though they did not bother adding that increased criminal law enforcement will result in more individuals being deprived of their firearms rights. Each year since 1994, the House Appropriations Committee has explicitly refused funding for ATF to process firearms restoration applications, although Congress has declined to address the substance of the statute and regulation allowing them, so on the books it appears that firearms owners have some relief straight from ATF when, in reality, they do not.

It is a painful irony that Congress has seen fit to expand the scope of firearms disqualifications in this same time period, including adding the misdemeanor domestic violence prohibition that was also slipped into an appropriations bill, while at the same time depriving firearms owners of a reasonable avenue of relief.

4

Attacking Noncriminal Disqualifications

Once you are familiar with the nine federal firearms disqualifiers and have received the statement of reasons for your Brady denial, it is time to determine the best course of action to take to overturn your denial. These will most likely include some combination of filing an administrative Brady appeal and attacking the disqualifying record in the original jurisdiction. We'll start with some tips and techniques for attacking disqualifications that are not criminal convictions.

THE ORDINARY ERROR: MISTAKEN IDENTITY

Mistakes do happen, and sometimes your Brady denial results from nothing more than mistaken identity. Your name may be the same as an alias used by someone wanted for a serious crime, or you may have the same name and birth date as someone who meets one of the other disqualifications. I've represented several individuals whose records were confused with those of a twin brother, or with a person of the same name and birth date who lived nearby or in a town in another state with a similar name (how many people named Joe Smith went to Kennedy High School in, say, Pleasantville or Middleton?).

Despite what you've heard about the burden of proof being on the government in criminal cases, when you are attempting to over-turn a Brady denial, the burden of proof is on you to show that the government was wrong. In a mistaken identity denial, you will have to first obtain the written statement of reasons as to why you received a denial. A simple administrative appeal filed with support-ing fingerprints and photographs should settle the matter. If you know an amenable local law enforcement officer who can supple-ment your appeal with a statement assuring that they've looked at the record of denial, and you are not the person in question, it can't hurt.

Denials for mistaken identity can be infuriating, since you have not done a single thing wrong, but fortunately they can also be easy to correct.

If your Brady denial was due to the fact that your name and other identifying information is similar to that of another person who is prohibited from possessing a firearm, you may expect to receive a delay or denial every time you try to buy a gun. NICS is precluded by law from maintaining records of Brady transactions that are approved for more than 24 hours, so every time an FFL calls in your information from a Form 4473, you are likely to go through the same denial process. In December 2004, NICS began a Voluntary Appeal File (VAF) program to give gun buyers an option for avoiding unnec-essary delays or denials. The VAF is a separate NICS database of approved firearms purchasers. If you request to be placed in the VAF, you will have to complete an application, available from the NICS appeals office, and submit fingerprint cards. NICS will then issue you a Unique Personal Identifier Number (UPIN). For the moment, you will need to write this number into Block 18a of Form 4473 every time you purchase a new firearm. In the near future, the 4473 will be revised to have a special place for the UPIN. While the VAF program means that NICS will maintain a permanent record of the fact that you are a firearms purchaser, it also means you can avoid needless hassles every time you buy a gun.

DISHONORABLE MILITARY DISCHARGE

A Brady denial on the grounds of dishonorable military dis-charge is probably the most difficult to overturn. The place to start is with your military discharge papers. If you didn't keep them or can't find them, request another copy from the appropriate branch of the armed services. If this proves to be a bureaucratic nightmare, the constituent services people at your Congressional representative or senator's office can be a big help.

There are numerous grades of discharge from the military, but only the lowest dishonorable discharge disqualifies you from firearms possession. Some Brady denials are in error because they are based on one of the modes of military discharge that fall between honorable and dishonorable. All intervening levels of medical and administrative discharge do not disqualify you (although a medical discharge for a mental health matter might—see below). If your discharge papers say something other than dishonorable discharge, obtain a certified copy of the discharge papers (again, your congressman's office can help) and submit it with your appeal.

If your discharge papers erroneously say dishonorable discharge, you will have to first correct that record through the administrative processes set by the branch of the military you served in. You will want to hire an attorney skilled in the rules and procedures of your branch of the military to do this. The people at NICS are not going to hear your arguments as to why your discharge should not be considered dishonorable.

Another avenue to check is whether your discharge or any actions that were the subject of a court-martial have received a pardon. Even if you have not personally received a pardon, at various points in our history, presidents have issued blanket pardons for various military issues, and your discharge may be covered by that pardon. If your discharge is not covered, but was for circumstances similar to those receiving blanket presidential pardons, you may still have success applying for an individual presidential pardon.

If you cannot obtain relief through your branch of the military service, and are denied a pardon, you are truly not likely to be successful with an administrative appeal. If you wish to pursue attacking your Brady denial to its last ends, federal court would be your only remaining option, but I do have to warn you that getting a federal court to overturn a decision that neither your military branch nor the president would overturn is an exceedingly long shot.

47

JUDICIAL DETERMINATION
OF MENTAL INCOMPETENCE

Over the next several years, Brady denials on the grounds of judicial determination of mental incompetence are likely to become a popular source of litigation and public controversy. Medical records are required by law to be kept under strict confidence; this is why this category of grounds for denial can only depend upon judicial determination of mental incompetence, not on a hospital or medical determination. However, the overlapping spheres of jurisdiction between the judiciary and medical personnel are often gray and blurred when it comes to mental status.

For example, criminal defendants are often deemed incompetent to stand trial at some point in their proceedings. This determination means that due to any number of various stressors—including physical rather than mental illness, or communication difficulties—they cannot meaningfully assist their counsel in the preparation of their defense at that time. Often, after the passage of time, the person is deemed competent again and the criminal justice proceedings move forward. Is a determination of temporary incompetence to stand trial the same thing as an adjudication of mental incompetence or defect? ATF regulations indicate that a finding of incompetence to stand trial disqualifies you from possessing firearms, but the question of whether the trial court's later overturning of the finding of incompetence changes your status under the Gun Control Act is yet to be litigated. If this is the basis for your denial, you are likely headed to federal court litigation to resolve it. If the trial court's finding of incompetence in your case was based on physical fatigue or physical condition, or some other personal disability rather than a mental health issue, you should have a strong argument for overturning your Brady denial in a federal court action.

Recently the Veterans Administration uploaded tens of thousands of records of Vietnam-era veterans who received medical military discharges due to mental health conditions such as battle fatigue or post-traumatic stress syndrome. Apparently, by regulatory fiat, the VA and NICS have determined that a mental health medical military discharge constitutes an adjudication of mental incompe-

48

tence. It remains to be seen whether the VA and NICS impose a similar conclusion on Gulf War I and II veterans' records.

Because the legal status of these denials is currently vague, it will take a number of courageous citizens willing to take on NICS and the VA to challenge denials through the federal court system in order for the law to become established as to what constitutes a proper Brady denial for this disqualification. With more and more records being made available to federal law enforcement through broad-sweeping powers such as those granted by the Patriot Act, we can expect this category of denial to increase dramatically in the coming years and new methods of challenging it to develop over time.

To challenge a mental health disqualification, obtain a complete, certified copy of the records of the hearings that resulted in the finding that NICS is basing the disqualification on. Carefully compare the exact words of the order or finding in the hearings to the ATF definitions for this disqualification. Was the court order that sent you to a mental health institution a request for observation or evaluation, or were you sent there because of a finding of mental defect or incompetence? Did the court accept your representation that you would voluntarily commit yourself to a drug or alcohol rehab program, or did the court involuntarily order you to attend such a program? These small details may be difficult to pull out of the trial court file, or tapes or transcripts of the hearings if they are available, but they make the difference between a Brady denial that will be upheld and one that can be overturned by the federal courts. Where interpretation of facts on the record of a prior trial court are involved, going to federal court is likely to be the best bet for overturning your denial.

KNOWN DRUG USER

A Brady denial on the grounds of being a "known drug user" is right up with denials based on dishonorable military discharges in terms of difficulty of reversal. Fortunately, it is also among the least common denial grounds now that Brady background checks have gone to NICS. Under the original Brady check system, CLEO, anyone the local officers considered an undesirable was likely to be labeled a "known drug user."

49

This classification of denial is unique in that it does not require even a single piece of evidence demonstrating that the individual is a "known drug user," nor does the law specify by whom such facts are to be "known." Today under NICS, the person conducting the background check looks to records on file and is not likely to be personally acquainted with the subject of the Brady check, so the odds of being labeled a "known drug user" based solely on appearance or aura of disrespectability are slimmer.

Still, all criminal records have a section in which the local law enforcement officer can insert various categories of information about a person: whether they have tattoos, whether they are believed to have gang affiliations, their religion, or other personal data, including believed drug or alcohol abuse or addiction status. It is still conceivable that individuals with minor criminal records, such as traffic tickets, that would not otherwise disqualify them from firearms ownership, would result in a Brady denial if a law enforcement officer somewhere along the way inserted "known drug user" into the criminal record data.

Under the CLEO system, I received numerous calls from individuals who had received Brady denials on these grounds. However, none of these individuals were willing or able to take the necessary steps to go to court and challenge the local law enforcement assertion that they were known drug users. It's uncomfortable to take your own small-town police chief to court over his or her perception of you, knowing that you and your family will continue to live there.

Reversing a Brady denial on these grounds will almost inevitably require litigation. I would recommend challenging the constitutionality of the denial, since the determination of "known drug user" does not meet due process standards of notice and opportunity for hearing before the determination is made. This is also a viable challenge if the disqualification was based on arrests that did not lead to convictions. There remains at least the theory in our criminal justice system that a person who is arrested remains innocent until proven guilty in a court of law; therefore, despite the ATF regulations to the contrary, it seems right to challenge a Brady denial based on charges that never resulted in a conviction.

If you are attacking a disqualification based on the "known drug user" grounds, you should also be prepared—to the extent that one can prove a negative—to submit some evidence indicating that you are not a drug user. This could be testimony of others, voluntary blood or urine tests, results of testing done at a place of employment, or any other means you can think of to demonstrate to a court's satisfaction that the conclusion that you are a drug user is erroneous.

It also remains to be seen how this disqualification will relate to persons who lawfully use medical marijuana—or who use prescription drugs surreptitiously brought in from Canada.

Because attacking a denial based on the grounds of being a "known drug user" will be based on facts that are open to interpretation, you will have to present evidence and testimony to support your claims to have the best chance of overturning your denial in federal court, or by following one of the alternative methods of negotiating out of a denial suggested below.

DENOUNCED U.S. CITIZENSHIP

I have never seen a case reported or talked to an individual who received a Brady denial on these grounds. It would appear that to be considered to have "denounced" your U.S. citizenship, you would need to take steps beyond merely making a denigrating comment toward America. However, given the rapid increase in prescribed acts which are being considered "terrorist" and therefore akin to treasonous activities, it is hard to say where this disqualification will go in the next several years. My only suggestion on trying to attack a disqualification on these grounds is that indications of continuing to act as a citizen—say, voting in an election or serving on jury duty, perhaps even driving with a valid driver's license from one of the United States—should serve as evidence to negate an allegation of denouncing your citizenship. As with being a "known drug user," this disqualification is based on facts that can be open to interpretation, rather than records or clear-cut documentation. You are likely to have to support your claim with witnesses and testimony, so your best bet will be in federal court.

51

OUTSTANDING DOMESTIC RESTRAINING ORDER

The law regarding the issuance and extinguishment of a temporary restraining order (TRO) in domestic situations varies from state to state. (Even the terminology varies; some states call it an abuse prevention order, some a family court stay-away order.) Receiving a Brady denial on the grounds of an "open" TRO is very common. If the TRO is old or you believe it to be closed, the first step is to obtain a certified copy of the court's actual order in the case. If the order clearly has an end date on it, or if your state laws specify a date at which TROs expire, submission of that documentation in your Brady administrative appeal has a high chance of being successful.

It is worth first taking a side venture and ensuring that your state's own criminal record system reflects that the TRO against you is closed. Each state has its own method of obtaining this information or petitioning for correction of your state criminal history. Submitting certified records indicating the TRO was closed should result in your state database promptly noting that there is no longer an outstanding TRO against you.

Unfortunately, such clear-cut evidence that the pending TRO is closed is not always easy to get. Many states may not have end dates on the TRO, particularly on older TROs, and may not have had statutes specifying an expiration date. In such cases, you will have to go back into your state court and seek an order indicating that the TRO is closed. This will likely involve petitioning the court, setting a hearing for which the person who originally obtained the TRO is notified, and appearing at the hearing.

You should use the utmost discretion in stating the reasons for your petition. The fact that there is an outstanding court order against you that is detrimental and should no longer be in effect and no longer serves any lawful purpose should be adequate reason to close an old TRO. At least some judges will not want to hear that you are seeking closure of the TRO to obtain a gun. In any event, that is not something that I suggest placing on the record unless the court or cross-examining attorney's explicit question leaves you with no honest choice but to make that statement. I'm not suggesting that you hide your pride in being a firearms owner—but discretion is often the better part of valor.

Once you get the old TRO closed and the closure noted on your state's database, proceed with a Brady administrative appeal to ensure that the Brady denial is noted as overturned on your record. If you don't go through this step, but just go back to the gun store figuring that it's been taken care of, the record will show no grounds for denial, but there will be a "red flag" that says you've recently gotten a denial, and that can cause problems. Avoid the hassle and get the denial overturned through the administrative process first.

Not all domestic restraining orders "count" to prohibit you from possessing firearms. Carefully compare the procedures that were used in your case to the statutory prohibitions. If there was never a hearing of which you were notified, or if there were not actual findings made as listed in the statute, the order against you should not support a Brady denial even if it gets listed in the domestic restraining order database. Get certified copies of the documents that show that the disqualifying process wasn't followed, and submit them with your administrative Brady appeal.

5

Attacking Fugitive from Justice or Pending Charges Disqualifications

FUGITIVE FROM JUSTICE

Unlike the doctor in that great movie and television series, you don't have to actually be on the run, in hiding, and looking for the one-armed man who really committed the crime to be considered a fugitive. If there is an outstanding criminal charge or warrant for you in any jurisdiction, you are considered a fugitive from justice.

It is very easy to be the subject of an outstanding warrant without being aware of it. If you got a traffic ticket while on vacation, then forgot about it, or got cited into court coming out of a rock concert in the early 1970s but were in such a state of mind that you never realized it until eight years later, you could well be a "fugitive from justice."

In law school, a friend of mine had his car towed on a Friday night for illegal parking in Boston, and when he went to pick the car up, he was cuffed and shackled and held in jail until Monday. Turns out years before, when he'd been in undergraduate school in that city, he'd gotten a ticket for making an illegal turn. His car had broken down the next week and been junked with the ticket still in the glove box. When he hadn't paid it or showed up to traffic court, a warrant was issued, and years later he discovered he'd been running around the countryside as a fugitive from justice.

Law enforcement agencies have plenty to do without tracking

down people who have outstanding warrants for things like traffic tickets, fish and game violations, or many minor criminal matters. Generally these things only come to light if the person for whom there is an outstanding warrant comes to the attention of police in some other way—like having his car towed or going through a Brady background check.

The easiest way to resolve a Brady denial based on an outstanding warrant is to resolve the outstanding warrant. "Easy," however, is relative. Resolving that outstanding warrant, depending on what it's for and how old it is, may be expensive or painful. Some jurisdictions may just charge you an extra fine and be delighted to have the unexpected revenue come in; others may indeed treat you like a criminal and inflict upon you additional charges for failing to appear in court, protracted legal proceedings, or even jail time for what had originally been a $25 ticket.

Once you've received a Brady denial and learned that you have an outstanding warrant, however, it's time to face the music. Once the warrant has been brought to your attention, your failure to promptly resolve it is much more likely to lead to a punitive attitude on the part of the prosecutor and judge.

You may find yourself certain that the case that was brought up in the Brady check report as having an outstanding warrant has actually been closed. Often the warrant has been lifted already or was wrongly entered when you showed up late or on the wrong day for court; or is issued for the wrong person; or your name happens to be the same as someone else for whom there is a warrant. If so, obtain a certified copy of the record of your case. You are particularly looking for a copy of a judgment order, mittimus, or release from probation—anything that shows that the case was satisfactorily concluded.[1]

If the warrant is actually for someone else, or for someone falsely using your identity, the fingerprints that you submit with your Brady appeal should resolve the wrongful Brady denial. While stolen identity crimes are common, they usually do not survive even fairly superficial law enforcement scrutiny. I was once told by a police officer who had pulled me over for speeding that there was an outstanding warrant out for me for a serious crime—the warrant listed my exact name and date of birth when he'd called in my driver's license number. I waited by the side of the road while he made a few more inquiries, and within about 15 minutes he'd determined that the person for whom the warrant was issued is of a different race than I am, so I was free to go. The officer did warn me, however, that if I ever had to go through a background check for anything, I was likely to experience difficulty until this has been cleared up.

Once the outstanding warrant is resolved, go back and process an administrative Brady appeal to get a notation that the denial was overturned.

DEFERRALS OR FILED MATTERS

Most jurisdictions have local practices that, formally or informally, allow a person charged with a crime to enter a guilty plea, but judgment or sentencing is "deferred" to some later date. In some states this deferral period has a definite date on which it expires; if the person hasn't gotten into any additional trouble in the intervening time, the case is dismissed. However, in such states, the dismissal often doesn't make it into the record or never gets formally acted on, in which case you may wind up with a Brady denial because it appears that you have an outstanding open criminal case pending. This will necessitate going back to the original court and getting the case marked as closed, then getting that closure reported to the state's criminal records agency. Sometimes you can make this happen with just a letter; other times it will require a court hearing.

In some states—in my practice, I've seen this most often in Massachusetts—cases are routinely noted as "filed." Unlike a formal deferral process, where the conviction is delayed for a set period of time, a case that is filed in Massachusetts just sits around indefinitely listed as an open matter. These open-but-filed cases cause problems in many legal proceedings.

If you are the victim of one of these filed notations on your record, you've got little choice but to either accept the Brady denial or go back and petition the court to close your filed case. Depending on the type of case, why it was filed, and how long ago it occurred, this could result in opening quite a can of worms. Unfortunately, neither NICS nor the federal court is going to listen to all the great reasons why that old filed or deferred matter shouldn't be held against you—the Gun Control Act relies on the states to determine what is or is not a conviction, and they can't decide to ignore notations on your state criminal record. You'll have to weigh the costs, advantages, and disadvantages of pursuing this option.

If you succeed at getting the filed or deferred case closed in a manner that does not look like a conviction, check with the court to make sure that it got sent to your state criminal records department, then process an administrative Brady appeal.

FAILURE TO ENTER FINAL DISPOSITION

In the "olden days"—back all of 10 years ago in many rural jurisdictions—when records were still kept on paper or index cards in handwritten ink, it was not uncommon for the final disposition of a case to miss being reported over to the state criminal records department. In recent years, as data entry firms have been hired to type decades of these handwritten records into NICS-accessible data bases, it has not been uncommon to find files where the final disposition was simply not entered, either on the handwritten form due to clerical error or in transcribing the form to the database, because the handwriting was illegible, or the entry was made in the wrong slot on the form, or the final index card simply got lost in the shuffle. This is probably one of the most common Brady denial errors.

To correct this mistake, you will need to obtain certified copies of your original court file. Be sure to get the *complete* file. Read the court documentation carefully, looking for the points that show that the case reached a final conclusion. This may be a notation that you entered a guilty plea, evidence of a trial, or an order of judgment. Sometimes these things appear as very small notations—just the letter "G" in a tiny box that says "plea" or "judgment." You may also find something called a mittimus, or a sentencing order. If either one of these things is there, it means there was a final judgment entered. Another thing you might find is an order sending you to probation and then, if luck is running with you, something indicating that you were released from probation.

If the notation in your file is quite clear regarding the case closure, simply send along certified copies of the record with your administrative appeal. In your administrative appeal letter, point out the places in the record where it shows the final disposition of the case.

If the notation is a little hazy or involves piecing together several different bits of information, see if you can get a court clerk or some other authoritative person to write you a letter documenting how the items in the file indicate that the case is closed. You may need to petition the original court to certify that the case is closed; this is more of a hassle but may result in a nice gold-sealed court order stating that the matter is concluded, which would look awfully nice in your Brady appeals letter package. Getting back into that original court may be tricky, however; another option is that most states have a means of petitioning a higher court for what's called "extraordinary matters," meaning things that don't fit into any other kind of category on the court schedule. An attorney familiar with your local court practices can help you with this.

Once you get that letter or order, send it off in a Brady administrative appeal (be sure to keep copies for your records first!), and you should be able to overturn your denial. If NICS decides that it's still too confusing, they may deny your appeal and you may have to go to federal court with it, but with strong documentary evidence, the odds of overturning your Brady denial are good.

ENDNOTE

1. A *judgment order* is the entry of a judgment of guilty or not guilty by the court; this would come after either a jury verdict or an entry of a plea agreement and stipulated plea. A *sentencing order* is then the order of the court imposing a particular sentence. It may or may not be an actual part of the judgment order; usually not, particularly in serious matters, because sentencing usually occurs at some period of time after the conviction and enter of judgment of guilty. A *mittimus* is, technically speaking, an order of a court to a sheriff or other appropriate law enforcement agent to transport a convicted person to a jail, prison, asylum, or other institution of incarceration; and it is also an order to the director of that institution to receive and safely keep the prisoner for a certain period of time or until additional operation of law deems otherwise. Some courts, either by practice or by accident, skip the separate sentencing order and just do a judgment and then a mittimus. So if a person is looking for sentencing records in his case, he needs to look for documents with any of these names. Also, it's not unusual (justice is an extremely imperfect system) for the sentencing order and mittimus to have different sentencing information on it. Sometimes these discrepancies can be used to help muddy the waters in terms of whether an incident is viewed as a felony or a misdemeanor.

6

Attacking Felony Conviction Disqualifications

Felony conviction is the most common basis for a Brady denial—and the most commonly overturned. Records regarding criminal convictions are often wrong or are misinterpreted either by the people who typed the records into the state criminal records database or by the people at NICS or your POC. Even if you know that you do have some kind of criminal conviction, don't assume that the Brady denial for it is correct. Carefully go through each of the points and details outlined below to see if the denial was in error. Then, even if the denial was legally correct, there may still be ways to attack the original conviction and get your Brady denial overturned.

GET THE COMPLETE FILE

If the reason stated for your Brady denial is a prior conviction that qualifies as a felony for federal purposes, your first step is to obtain the complete court file for the case. Depending on how old the conviction is, you may need to get the file either from the original court or from a public records agency or state archives. If it is in state archives, you may need to spend some number of hours looking for it on microfiche or microfilm, or more recently on some sort of scanned digital records. If there is an option for looking at the original paper records, do so. Often, not everything from the file makes it onto microfiche, or only a portion of the page is readable.

Or there may be critical, pencil-written notes on the original papers that don't show up on the microfiche version.

Be sure to get the complete court record for the entire case including the original charging document, docket sheets, clerk's entries, filings, plea agreements, mittimus, and release for probation or parole. The devil of overturning Brady denials is in the details, and you never know quite which piece of paper will hold the detail critical to your case.

Unless you have a distinct recollection of the event and court case, the first thing you'll have to do is determine if in fact you are the right person. Most people presume that someone with a serious criminal conviction remembers the event. However, this seems to not be the case at least 10 percent of the time. I've had many clients convicted of things, such as felony trespass (one in which a guy on a road trip snuck into a church parsonage to use the shower) or lewd and lascivious behavior (for, say, urinating in public at a concert) between the years 1968 and 1975, who have no recollection of the incident or charges whatsoever.

And as these real-life examples show, not all "felonies" are anything that you'd consider a serious crime. When the general public talks about convicted felons, the image they hold is usually of a murderer, rapist, arsonist, or terrorist. The truth is, most convicted felons are convicted of property crimes or drug crimes, many of which are awfully minor. There is a large difference between a felony and a violent crime or a capital crime such as murder, rape, or arson. The firearms prohibition for persons convicted of a crime with a sentence of one year or more applies to people all the way down to teenagers who stole a stereo worth more than the state's prescribed felony level (usually $100); or, in one case that I had, an unemployed mother who stole more than $50 worth of groceries to feed her family. Most convicted felons are pretty darn ordinary people, and most felonies are not the kinds of crimes that would lead most citizens to think that the perpetrator should be forever barred from hunting or serving in the armed forces or joining the police force.

Brady denials occur for criminal convictions going as far back as records were kept. A few years ago I saw a man in his later years receive a Brady denial for a conviction that had occurred during a bar fight when he was home on leave from the service—in World War II. The judge had lined all the boys up, given them a lecture, then sent them back out to the war. This man had served his country then lived honorably for decades, raising a family, running a business, and contributing to his community. He had never realized that when his army buddies and the line of navy guys on the other side of the room had nodded their aching heads and apologized for their unseemly behavior, that the judge had entered assault convictions on every one of their records, merely waiving the sentence, not the charges. Receiving the news that he was really a convicted felon came as quite a bit of a shock to him.

But unless you get the complete copy of the court file for the incident referred to in the statement of reasons for your Brady denial, you will not know for sure that your case really was classified as a felony or be able to begin to pick it apart for errors or avenues of attack.

IS IT YOU?

If you don't recall the criminal incident—or even if you think you do—check the case record very carefully and determine if it is you being talked about. Check the address at the time of the charge, the age, date of birth, and any other identifying information such as a Social Security number. Then, check the information on your court record very carefully against the case information given to you in the statement of reasons for your Brady denial. Is it the same case? Are you the person listed in the conviction? Don't laugh—it is fairly common to wind up with a conviction record due to someone else with a similar name. And I've represented three different sets of clients involving twins, where the criminal records were confused between the two of them, even listing the other twin's name as an alias on the criminal history documents.

If the person convicted is not you, send a certified copy of the relevant documents together with the best evidence you can locate on the point of difference—an old driver's license showing your address at the time of the case, your Social Security card, a birth certificate—and send them in with your Brady appeal. If this does not result in overturning your Brady denial, you will need to present the same evidence in federal court. But before you file the lawsuit, try sending the information and documentation to your local office of ATF and the local prosecuting Assistant U.S. Attorney with a cover letter advising that the Brady denial was in error, based on an incorrect identification in the criminal records. This just may resolve the issue short of an actual lawsuit.

DOES THE CONVICTION MEET THE DEFINITION?

Whether you served jail time, paid a fine, or were even on probation does not determine whether any particular criminal conviction disqualifies you from possessing firearms under the federal statute. Unless it is obvious that your conviction constitutes a felony under federal law (murder, armed robbery), you need to carefully determine whether, at the time of your conviction, the charges you were convicted under bore a potential penalty of more than one year in jail, or were considered a state misdemeanor but bore a potential penalty of more than two years in jail.

It is critical to find an accurate copy of the statute you were convicted under *as it was in effect at the time of your conviction*. Our society has gotten increasingly punitive over the last 30 years. Many actions that were considered misdemeanors have been turned into felonies; many infractions like fish and game tickets or traffic tickets have been turned into misdemeanors and have punishments that work their way into the felony category as well.

Bicycle theft, joyriding, and possession of small, personal consumption amounts of drugs such as marijuana have crept up the criminal punishment ladder to become considered serious crimes. Just as family fights that were once treated as disorderly conduct or with a disturbance ticket now count effectively as felonies because they are "crimes of domestic violence," possessing a joint is now considered a serious drug crime, and hunting violations are often considered "weapons crimes." Juveniles are increasingly charged as adults, and courts do not hesitate to write a felony conviction on to the criminal record of a teenager, despite the fact that it will preclude him from getting college loans, government business contracts, travel visas, or FHMA mortgages for the rest of his life. The theft of, say, a lawn ornament is no longer greeted with the wry observation that boys will be boys. It is instead as often as not treated as a criminal matter bearing lifelong impact.

Before adoption of the Gun Control Act of 1968, it effectively did not matter whether a person's conviction was for a misdemeanor or a felony. Some states did have voting or jury disqualifications back then for people with felony convictions, but many of those states were still wrestling with issues of extending voting rights to all citizens regardless of race, literacy, or other factors. Additionally, with only index-card or paper ledger criminal records, it was not possible to tell if a person who just moved in from another state had a prior felony conviction.

When the Gun Control Act of 1968 went into effect, local law enforcement developed a heightened awareness of who had prior felony convictions and who didn't. In states that value their hunting traditions, or where a firearm is a necessary tool of rural living, courts either went through pains to avoid imposing a felony conviction except in egregious cases, or they simply chose to ignore the prohibitions of the Gun Control Act of 1968 unless the person engaged in potentially dangerous behavior. Here in Vermont, local law enforcement agencies and the court exercised large doses of case-by-case discretion, adopting an informal policy that if a guy with a prior felony conviction kept hunting rifles and did not engage in violent acts, he would not be charged with federal gun laws violations. If that guy brought himself to the attention of law enforcement authorities with a new crime, then he might have to face the federal law issue.

Your prior conviction might have come from a court that went through pains to not impose felonies on people. Or it might have come from a court where no one paid much attention to whether something was a felony or not, because as a practical matter it made no impact one way or the other. You will only know whether your conviction was for a misdemeanor or a felony by carefully researching the statute as it existed at the time of your conviction.

In this digital information age, written laws are becoming more accessible to everyone because you can just look them up on the Internet instead of drudging through a dusty old law library. In fact, even law libraries are increasingly ditching their books, which take up valuable real estate space, in favor of digital files.

The problem with this is that it is getting increasingly hard to find anything other than the current version of a statute. There are many reasons why a person might need to find an actual copy of, say, what the marijuana possession statute was in New Jersey in 1967. If that person is convicted of a new federal crime, his jail sentence will depend on whether that 1967 conviction was a felony or a misdemeanor. And if that person wants to buy a new hunting rifle, his right to possess firearms will also ride on how that 1967 conviction was classified at the time he was convicted.

If you still live in the state where you got the original conviction, I suggest going to your state law library or the nearest law school library and asking for help finding the statutes for the year of your conviction from the reference librarian. If the library no longer keeps these back statutes, your next step is to find someone called the state archivist. The state archivist will be thrilled to hear from you because state archivists almost never get phone calls from the public. With any luck, the state archivist will take on the task of finding your old statute like a knight on a quest.

If the state archivist is unsuccessful, your next avenue will be the records of the state legislature. You can probably find the original "sessions laws" version of the statute buried in the minutes or records of the legislature, although this may involve paging through many volumes of records going back from the date of your conviction, depending on how well they are indexed. You might see if you can talk a law student into helping you out with this. (For some inexplicable reason, law students find paging through old legislative books exciting.)

I was once searching for an old version of a Florida state statute regarding joyriding. My client had received a Brady denial because today, joyriding in Florida (operating without owner's consent) is a felony. But my client was absolutely certain that at the time he was convicted—decades ago, when he was 16—it was a misdemeanor. Fortunately the Florida state law librarian was extremely helpful. Although we could not find an actual set of statutes from the year of my client's conviction, the librarian found one from two years prior and one from one year after the target date. She sent both copies along with a letter stating that she'd searched the records and there was no indication that there had been any changes in this law in the intervening years. My client's Brady denial was overturned at the administrative appeal level, thanks to the librarian.

Another confusing issue arises when the statute or the criminal justice practice of the jurisdiction where you were convicted allowed prosecutors to charge a crime as either a misdemeanor or a felony. I have seen numerous old conviction records where the statute seems to indicate the charge was at least potentially a felony, but the court case record indicates it was a misdemeanor. Some old court records don't even have a place where it could be indicated whether the charge was a felony or misdemeanor. In such cases you will have to read every piece of paper in the court records very carefully. This may not be the easiest job depending on the handwriting of the clerks involved and the copy quality of the public records. Remember, absence of a reference to a "felony" is not enough; the burden is on you to prove that the government is wrong in concluding that your conviction is a felony. You must be the one to prove that it's a misdemeanor. You are looking for the word "misdemeanor" or the letter "M" attached anywhere to the charges anywhere in your court file.

If you are charged with something that could have been either a misdemeanor or a felony, and you cannot find a designation on your court record, you are likely to have to either accept your Brady denial or dig further. You can either dig out—by going back to the public records archives and reading through file after file, looking for other cases for the same charges in the time period around your conviction, hoping that one of them will contain a misdemeanor reference—or you can dig down—submitting letters or whatever open-records applications your state may have seeking court and prosecutor file memos or policies from that time period discussing how they treated cases like yours. The more documentation and record evidence in your favor that you can gather at this stage, the better.

There hasn't been any case law that I've seen on this point yet, but if you challenge a Brady denial in federal court where your criminal history file and all your research simply can't determine whether your conviction was for a felony or a misdemeanor, I'd suggest arguing the rule of lenity; this rule of federal common law indicates that directly conflicting points of criminal law must be resolved in favor of the criminal defendant (kind of a tie-goes-to-the-runner situation). If there is no direct evidence that the state of conviction intended to ensure that you were convicted of a felony, you should certainly argue that you are entitled to a presumption that the more lenient option—that of a misdemeanor conviction—should be applied. If the judge in your federal district court likes academic arguments, he or she just might overturn your Brady denial on those grounds.

HAS THE CONVICTION BEEN TAKEN BACK OUT OF DISQUALIFICATION?

If all your research and analysis of your court file and the statutes at the time of your conviction indicate that you are indeed convicted of a felony, your attack on your Brady denial is not necessarily over. Not all disqualifying criminal convictions remain that way.

Hundreds of thousands of felony convictions come back out of their disqualifying status because of the administrative policies of the convicting state. This is to the advantage of those hundreds of thousands of people looking to restore their firearms rights, but it also points out one of the largest unjust impacts of the federal firearms laws: A 35-year-old man convicted of armed robbery in one state may soon be legally hunting or carrying a sidearm again; a 17-year-old boy convicted of stealing a bicycle in another state may be precluded from possessing a firearm for the rest of his life. The federal disqualification depends on the criminal procedures of the state in which the person was convicted, and has nothing whatsoever to do with the nature of the crime for which the person was convicted.

Under the federal gun control law, if you had certain fundamental civil rights taken away from you by virtue of your conviction, and then those rights were reinstated later—either automatically by virtue of the fact that you were released from probation or parole, or in response to an application process—then your conviction no longer counts as meeting the federal disqualifying definition. That means you can have your guns, even with a prior felony conviction, depending on what state it was in, when it happened, and what the state rules were relative to your case.

Federal court case law has begun to narrow the definition of which civil rights count for this exemption from disqualification. Most courts have held that being deprived of your liberty, for instance, doesn't count, so the mere fact that you served jail time and then were released does not undo the disqualification. I tried to argue to one federal court that the fact that you couldn't have guns while on felony probation was a civil right that was taken away—but I lost. Most courts now agree that the civil rights intended by this phrase of the statute are your right to vote, to serve on a jury, or to hold public office.

Ironically, if your conviction is from a state such as Vermont, which does not take away any of the rights of its convicted criminals, then those rights can never be reinstated. Despite the state's intent to not take away any of the rights of citizenship for those people whom it convicts of crimes, the federal government then takes away one of those citizens' most treasured rights—the right to bear arms.

If your conviction was from a state that precludes persons convicted of a felony from voting while they are in jail or on parole, but then restores that voting right on release from parole or probation, your right to bear arms has also been restored. A certified copy of the release document that states that your voting rights have been reinstated, or a copy of the statute from the time of your conviction demonstrating that reinstatement of voting rights was law, should either succeed on your administrative Brady appeal or be successful in restoring your rights in federal court.

LEGAL ATTACKS ON THE ORIGINAL CONVICTION

If you are the right person referred to in the Brady denial, and your conviction is for a crime that meets the federal disqualification definition, and your conviction was not removed from disqualification because you had civil rights removed and restored, the next thing to do is determine if the conviction could be subject to legal attack in the originating court.

A good place to start is to carefully check what your age was at the time of the incident for which you were convicted and at the time of the conviction. If you were under 22 years old on either of these dates, take the time to research what your state's definition of the age of majority was on those dates.

Many states have changed the age of majority back and forth from 18 to 21 on several occasions. If you were under the age of majority at the time of your criminal charges, you were probably entitled, or possibly required, to have a parent or court-appointed guardian present. If you did not, your conviction may not meet the federal definition of a disqualifying conviction. Alternatively, you may be able to go back into the court in which you received the conviction and challenge it in a post-conviction relief petition for having been unlawfully entered if you were a minor without a guardian or lawyer present.

I have sometimes seen a juvenile court conviction erroneously entered into the criminal history records. If your conviction was supposed to be considered a juvenile court matter, you can petition the original court to have the file sealed—and you may even be able to sue them for the cost of representation on your Brady appeal because it may well have been a juvenile records privacy violation to disclose your juvenile record to NICS or the POC.

In most states, if you were charged with a crime as an adult before you reached the age of majority, you may be able to get the record either sealed or expunged.

As with trying to find a copy of the statute under which you were convicted at the time of said conviction, finding your state's laws regarding the age of majority at the time of your conviction can be long, dusty work. Follow the same process outlined above for contacting your state law librarian or archivist for assistance.

Next, research whether the statute under which you were convicted was ever overturned in your state due to later declarations that the law or processes used were illegal. If your state's highest court overturned the statute you were convicted under, you may be able to go back into court and petition to overturn your conviction.

Consult with a skilled criminal defense appellate attorney about any other avenues available in your state for attacking the original conviction. Were you represented by counsel, or did you legally waive your right to counsel? Were there other errors in the course of your case that could be challenged under your state's laws or constitution? Every state has different rules and procedures for reopening an old conviction, and every case will have different odds of success.

As a long shot, review whether you received specific advice regarding the impact of the conviction on your firearms rights. If you were not told by your attorney that the conviction would disqualify you from firearms possession, you may be able to bring a post-conviction relief motion for ineffective assistance of counsel. However, this only works for firearms disqualifications that were on the books at the time of your conviction. I have received dozens of calls from people who were not advised by their attorneys 20 years ago that their misdemeanor domestic convictions would disqualify them from firearms possession—but their attorneys could not possibly have predicted that this state of affairs would come to pass in 1998.

EXPUNGEMENT AND PARDON

Two other options for removing the original conviction are the processes of expungement and pardon (also called clemency or executive clemency).

Almost every state has some process of expunging a criminal conviction, which means that you receive a court order effectively wiping the conviction off your record. In a few states, such as Vermont, this process is only available for convictions that occurred when you were a juvenile.

Each state that has this process requires a different period of time to elapse before you are eligible to apply for expungement, and most of these states have a set procedure for applying for it. You can expect to have to provide documentation and letters or testimony showing that you have led a productive, peaceful life without violating the state's laws since the time of your original conviction. In some states, expungement is either automatic or fairly routine after a certain period of time has passed for most nonviolent offenses. In other states, expungement is purely discretionary, in the hands of the judge to either grant or deny for nearly any reason or none at all.

Pardon, or executive clemency as most states now call it, means that the governor of the state in which you got the conviction officially forgives you for the incident. Clemency can be complete, having the same effect as an expungement in wiping the conviction off your record, or clemency can be incomplete, reserving certain specified detrimental effects of the pardon. I have seen governor's pardons that state that they deem the conviction to be null and void except for purposes of the federal gun control laws—meaning even though you are pardoned, you still can't have your firearms.

Every state has some sort of pardon board; it is often the same group of people as the parole board. Most states have a formal application procedure for pardons.

Both pardons and expungements usually require that you show that your record has been absolutely clean since the disqualifying conviction; that you have led what the parole boards like to call "an orderly and industrious life" since your criminal incident; and that you have the kinds of friends, family, and community ties that indicate that you are well grounded and responsible. Be prepared to show that you completed school; have a job; have raised your kids to do well; are part of a religious or charitable organization; have done good deeds in your community; and deeply regret the past criminal incident. Coming into a pardon or expungement hearing proclaiming that you never should have been convicted because that some-bee who charged you was a lying dog is not likely to advance your cause. It's usually wise to show the court or pardon board a heavy dose of humility and respect, no matter how frustrating the process or pointed the questions you receive. Often, the frustrations they dish your way are a means of testing you—if you lose your temper, you'll fail the test.

Expungements and, particularly, governor's pardons, seem to be getting fewer and farther between. We live in an era of fear that "something might happen"; any governor looking at a pardon application is thinking to him or herself, if this person goes out and commits a crime after I pardoned him, it will not go well in my next election. This is why a statistically substantial number of pardons gets written by lame-duck governors who have already been voted out of office but whose terms are not yet up.

In some states, it helps to cultivate political friends and a working awareness of the politics of the governor's office, perhaps even waiting until the right administration comes along, before applying for your pardon. When you are getting letters of support for your pardon or expungement application, it certainly doesn't hurt if you get letters from names that will be recognized by the governor or parole board. This isn't corruption as much as it's human nature—if someone known to these people will vouch for you, it will carry a substantial impact on the decision-makers. If you don't know such people, don't sweat it—look to your boss, guys from the firehouse where you volunteer, friends from church, your kid's schoolteachers, and parents on the Little League team that you coach.

There are several great Web sites that have catalogued all the states' pardon and expungement procedures.

Two to try are:

- http://www.uslawbooks.com/books/state
- http://www.uslegalforms.com/lawdigest/
  expungement-of-criminal-records-law.htm

The processes can also be found on your own state's Web sites if you search under terms like "expungement," "expunction," "pardon," and "clemency." It is usually not necessary to have an attorney represent you during an expungement or pardon process; however, if you are not overly confident of your writing skills, or if government forms and hearings make you nervous, you can hire an attorney to assist you. A less expensive option is simply to have an attorney look over your expungement or pardon application package once you have it assembled to see if you have everything together right and make suggestions on how to best proceed.

Some states have a process called sealing a record in addition to, or instead of, an expungement process. You will have to carefully check your state's laws regarding sealing records. Unlike an expungement, sealed cases don't completely disappear and can be opened and the conviction used for certain situations. In your state, this may or may not mean that sealing a record will remove it from Brady prohibition status. In many states, juvenile convictions and certain other classifications of convictions are supposed to be sealed automatically—but as with any large record-keeping system, sometimes this doesn't happen. If you've got juvenile adjudications of

73

delinquency or convictions, you would be wise to double-check with the court to ensure that the record has been properly sealed.

Once you obtain a pardon or expungement, ask the board issuing it if they will submit it to the state's criminal record database. If not, you will have to locate and submit a certified copy of the expungement or pardon yourself. Get several certified copies of this document; sending one along with a Brady administrative appeal should overturn your Brady denial as long as NICS or the POC can confirm the expungement or pardon with the right state office.

ALTERNATIVE APPROACHES

Winning a legal battle—such as getting your Brady denial over-turned—is a lot like hand-to-hand combat. It's great to have a powerful right hook, and sometimes you have to come in blasting. But other times, a little martial arts philosophy can better get you where you need to go—with less of a bloody nose in the process. Instead of taking the direct-confrontation approach, it can help to first try an easier route.

If you've determined that your conviction counts under the federal gun control law, and you are facing having to attack the conviction in the original court, consider approaching the prosecutor's office and trying to negotiate a retroactive amendment to the charge. Maybe that sounds strange—why would a prosecutor agree to go back and have your felony amended to a misdemeanor? Maybe because that same prosecutor is going to have to participate in the hearings when you present whatever attack you are going to make on the charge in court. They are going to have to track down the original police officers and victims or witnesses to see if they have objections to whatever legal action you file.

If it has been 15 years since your criminal charges and you've had no intervening charges, that prosecutor would much rather spend his time and resources on currently pending cases. He might just want to sign an agreement to get you gone. Or the prosecutor might suggest you just apply for an expungement or pardon—in which case you can reply that you take that to mean that he'd be happy to sign a letter stating that he has no objection to an expungement or pardon, which certainly can't hurt on your application. Of course he might simply say no (or even laugh), but you'll never know if you don't ask, and you may find yourself negotiating a resolution without ever getting to a big fight. If you're particularly lucky, your negotiated agreement may include language saying "this conviction doesn't trigger Brady."

You might, once again, want to exercise discretion regarding how much emphasis you put on stating that you want this felony gone because you want to have guns. The level of the discretion you may want to exercise on this point will vary depending on your state and on who your judge and prosecutor are. In many rural states, the prosecutor is likely to be a duck or grouse hunter himself and may even be amenable to helping a fellow sportsman get his guns back. Such country prosecutors are regrettably a dying breed, but I've negotiated a few firearms-friendly retroactive settlements with some of the last of them.

If you live in a jurisdiction that's not firearms-friendly, or if you are not certain of the perspective of the prosecutor or judge on firearms, it would do good to at least mention any of the dozens of other reasons why you'd want a criminal conviction off your record: ability to travel freely to Canada or other countries requiring travel visas; ability to get government contracting jobs; FMHA mortgages; government-backed student loans; and countless other opportunities that are not open to convicted felons. And there's always the reason that you just want to put it behind you and no longer be identified as the criminal that the conviction represents.

If the prosecutor is not amenable to negotiating a gentler resolution and there isn't a mechanism for directly reopening your case for attack due to the passage of time or the particulars of your state's criminal procedures, search your state statutes for some device such as a provision granting your superior court general equitable jurisdiction to hear all matters for which a person does not have relief elsewhere. Every state has at least one method to get your toe in the door and plead for mercy from the court if there seems to be no other avenue for a court remedy. It is usually called something like a "petition for extraordinary relief." If you can get to a court hearing, lay out your case: You have an old criminal conviction that you never assumed would later create these kinds of problems in your life, and now that you realize the onerous burden of the conviction, you are requesting relief. Be prepared to present a mini-version of a pardon or expungement presentation to the court. Since you'll be going in front of a judge or panel of judges on this one, it's likely a good idea to have an attorney represent you just to ensure that all the protocols of court appearances are followed.

Alternatively, your state constitution may make your legislature the state's court of last resort. You might find a friendly ear in a fish and game committee who will entertain a personal legislative bill restoring your firearms rights under state law. Surprisingly enough, legislatures—and especially Congress—pass private bills like this all the time. The trick is finding a committee that will hear it and get it out on the floor for a courtesy vote.

If you get an agreement amending your conviction in the original court, send certified copies of the amended record to your state criminal records division and NICS along with an administrative Brady appeal; this should result in your Brady denial being overturned. If you get something like a higher court equitable order or a legislative order, go ahead and try the NICS Brady appeal route, but because the documentation you will be presenting will be somewhat out of the ordinary, you may have to proceed to federal court in order to present testimony as to what the documents are and how they nullify your conviction.

Before going into a federal lawsuit, again try the negotiated settlement option. Most U.S. Attorney's offices have a particular person assigned to firearms laws matters, so you can count on that person to really know his stuff in this field. You might find an Assistant U.S. Attorney who really wants to play hardball and make you file suit—but, like local prosecutors, most of them have their hands full with really pressing current matters. If you've got a decent argument that your Brady denial was wrong and should be overturned—a decent enough argument that it's clear you're going to file suit and make this prosecutor go through investigation, discovery, and a trial when he's got active terrorist and drug smuggling cases in need of attention—you may well be able to work something out the quick way.

If you are having trouble fighting your Brady denial straight on, think about ways to get around the underlying disqualification instead. Sometimes neutralizing it rather than fighting it gets that denial overturned faster and easier.

7

Attacking Disqualifications for Misdemeanor Domestic Violence Convictions

The pattern for addressing prior misdemeanor crimes of domestic violence is similar to that of handling felony convictions, but the details are even more critical and there are a few more avenues for potentially successful administrative Brady appeals.

COMPARE AND CONTRAST

As with a felony conviction disqualification, the first thing you need to do is get a *complete* copy of the court records. If there were hearings held, or any kind of court appearance at all, you should also order copies of the tapes or transcripts of those hearings. Ordering transcripts can be time consuming, but you can sometimes get duplicate copies of the tapes or videotapes faster. To find out the best way to do this in your court, talk with the court clerks. And talk nice— court clerks can make your life easy, or they can make it miserable. And while clerks cannot, of course, take bribes, I have discovered that cookies somehow don't count as bribes.

Once you get that file, carefully compare the charge and the facts you were convicted of to the federal definition of a misdemeanor crime of domestic violence. Some abuse prevention order violations, and even some convictions under state domestic assault laws, do not meet the federal statutory definition. On the other hand, many disorderly conduct or simple assault convictions meet the federal definition of a misdemeanor crime of domestic violence, if the facts involved include an act of force and a family or household member.

You must review—with extreme attention to detail—the actual charging documents for the original charge and the details of any amendment concurrent with a plea or the facts that were offered at a plea agreement as basis for the plea. If you pled guilty, hopefully either your plea agreement or the tape or transcript of your change of plea hearing stated which facts or document you pled guilty on; if not, it is assumed that you are pleading guilty based on the facts in the original police officer's affidavit of probable cause that supported bringing the charge. If that original affidavit or police report includes facts that meet the federal gun control law definition of a misdemeanor crime of domestic violence, then you have a disqualifying conviction.

Often, depending on the state and the circumstances, the document or statement of facts that you are pleading guilty to is not the same as the original affidavit of probable cause or original police report. This is especially true if (a) your charge was originally for a felony and then amended to a misdemeanor or (b) if it was originally charged as something called a domestic assault, then amended to a disorderly conduct—both very common scenarios in a domestic argument situation. Again, it doesn't matter what the charge you were convicted of is *called*—what matters are the actual facts for which you were adjudged guilty.

If your conviction was by a judge or jury after trial, you may need to obtain the transcripts to determine precisely which facts were presented in testimony and evidence. Again, the facts presented at trial might well be different from those in the original police report. The facts you were convicted on are the ones that count.

If the underlying facts upon which the conviction was based as grounded in the charging or plea agreement documents do not meet the federal definition, incorporate that argument into your administrative Brady appeal. However, if you've got something labeled a misdemeanor domestic assault conviction, it is highly unlikely that you will get the NICS appeal to overturn the denial. You will probably be headed to federal court, although this is one scenario where writing to your local branch of ATF and your local U.S. District Attorney's office may work well. These folks are very knowledgeable about exactly what the federal gun control law and their regulations say; if you can show them that your conviction doesn't meet their regulations, you may well wind up being able to reach a reasonable resolution that won't waste the court's time—and anybody else's time and resources either.

If this does not result in a correction of your denial, you will have to bring a federal lawsuit to obtain relief. There are a lot of gray zones in this area of the law and not much case law has been reported yet determining the complete parameters of when various kinds of convictions meet the federal definition of misdemeanor crime of domestic violence. We can safely assume that those parameters will get more stringent as time goes by.

USING THE PROCEDURAL SAFEGUARDS

The misdemeanor crime of domestic violence disqualification contains two procedural safeguards that are not present in the felony conviction disqualification. The statute states that if you were not represented by an attorney (or did not knowingly and intelligently waive your right to counsel) or if you were not tried by a jury (or did not knowingly and intelligently waive your right to a jury trial), your conviction does not count for this prohibition.

It is somewhat ironic that these same safeguards do not apply to the felony conviction prohibition. If you were not represented by an attorney or not told about your right to a jury trial on a felony, your only recourse is to raise these issues back in the original court to try to nullify the conviction. But if you were not represented by an attorney or not told about your right to a jury trial on a misdemeanor charge of domestic violence, you can raise these issues in an administrative Brady appeal or in further appeal to federal court without going back to the original state court.

Does your criminal case record indicate that you were represented by legal counsel? If not, is there record of an affirmative waiver of your right to counsel? What about your right to a jury trial? If you weren't tried by jury—that is, if you entered a guilty or no-contest plea, or had a trial in front of a judge—is there a record of an affirmative waiver of your right to a jury trial?

79

You are likely to have to check the tapes or transcripts of the hearings in your case to be sure; these waivers, particularly in cases from many years ago, and particularly in places and at times where the misdemeanor crime of domestic violence was considered a pretty minor legal occurrence, these waivers were only done orally in the course of reading off some boilerplate questions at the time the judge accepted your plea agreement. But in such times and places, these waivers were also often not done at all.

Since the burden is on you to prove that you did not have counsel or were not apprised of your right to a jury trial, you will need to either submit an affidavit to this effect with your administrative Brady appeal or testify under oath if your appeal proceeds to federal court. If you remember being represented by an attorney or waiving your jury right, even if that fact is not clear in the documented court records, do not commit federal perjury by testifying that you weren't, because this can only result in additional federal charges. In such cases, consult with a federal criminal defense attorney to determine if there are other ways you can proceed, or rethink this avenue of attack on your Brady denial.

Because this question of whether you properly waived your rights to counsel and a jury is factually based, and because so many of these old domestic misdemeanors were treated in such a casual manner, this is likely to become over time a large area of challenges on Brady denials. So far, there is no clear case law or ATF regulation defining exactly what evidence will constitute proper proof on these points, but it is clear that you have the burden of proving that there wasn't a lawyer or a jury in your case.

This can be a tantalizingly frustrating safeguard, because in thousands of these older domestic misdemeanors, it is not possible to obtain the original court records. Historically, legal systems treated misdemeanors as no big deal. That's because, until this federal gun control prohibition came along in 1998, misdemeanors never *were* a big deal. Many thousands of people over the years have been told— rightly at the time—that having a misdemeanor conviction on their record was a small thing that would never affect their daily lives, and those same many thousands of people were likely advised to just pay the fine and not have to bother coming back to court again, with all its expense and inconvenience. These folks have a shocking feeling of injustice when all these years later they discover that this minor legal transaction now deprives them of their firearms rights. Yet, there has been no hue and cry set up against the law by firearms owners or their organizations. Instead, firearms owners who receive a Brady denial on these grounds are left to try to appeal their denials on a case-by-case basis.

REMOVAL AND RESTORATION OF CIVIL RIGHTS

It is important to conduct a detailed check of the state of conviction's practices regarding removal and restoration of civil rights *specifically for misdemeanors*. While many states have provisions that remove civil rights when a person is convicted of a crime and then restore those rights at a later date either automatically or after a petition and hearing process, those provisions often apply only to persons who are convicted of a felony or who have been jailed.

For example, there is case law regarding Michigan misdemeanor violence convictions indicating that where the person convicted had lost his right to vote while in prison and had that vote restored to him on release and was not prohibited by Michigan law from possessing a firearm, his federal firearms rights were restored and he could not be prosecuted for unlawful firearms possession.

It is much less likely to have gotten a sentence that involved any jail time when you've had a misdemeanor, rather than a felony, charge. But in domestic cases, it is pretty common for the person charged to be held overnight or over a weekend before being arraigned. Very carefully research your state's civil rights removal statutes and any case law on the subject, as well as the regulations of your state Department of Corrections and court administration rules, and see if you can support an argument that your rights were removed and then restored because you were held in jail, even if you were just held overnight while awaiting an initial court appearance. Submit certified copies of whatever supporting regulations you discover with your administrative Brady appeal or federal court appeal. If you wind up in federal court, you may need to subpoena an administrative official from your state government to explain the state's policy on this point. Ask the administrator this question when he is on the stand: If your domestic quarrel had occurred on the eve of election day and you were held in jail awaiting arraignment—would he have let you out to go vote?

PARDONS AND EXPUNGEMENTS: ATTACKING THE ORIGINAL CHARGE

If none of the approaches listed above get you a viable attack on a Brady denial for a misdemeanor crime of domestic violence, you may once again have to either attack the conviction in the original court or seek a pardon or expungement, following all the same processes and tips outlined above for felony convictions. Unfortunately, other than some states that have simpler expungement processes for misdemeanor convictions, it is bizarrely and significantly harder to get a court order overturning, or an expungement or a pardon on, a misdemeanor crime of domestic violence. In fact, some states, such as South Carolina, allow expungements for everything *but* crimes of domestic violence. If you rob a bank in South Carolina, or import heroin, you can apply for an expungement. If you had a domestic quarrel that wound up in front of a magistrate with a $25 fine 40 years ago—as many tens of thousands of people did—you can't.

In other states, there is no expungement or pardon available for a misdemeanor. Again, most state laws continue to operate on the theory that a misdemeanor wouldn't need to be pardoned or expunged, since having a misdemeanor on your record had virtually no effect on your daily life until the 1998 amendment to the federal gun control law.

In many aspects of the attack on a misdemeanor domestic Brady denial, it can be helpful if the domestic partner who was involved in the incident is supportive of your current efforts. Granted, it is often the case where either you no longer even know where this person is, or the two of you remain at loggerheads. If this is the case, don't go trying to pursue your former partner on this issue. But if by chance with the passage of time you've either repaired your relationship or gotten to be reasonably friendly, your partner's willingness to support your attempts to amend the original conviction or to overturn the Brady denial can go a long way toward persuading a prosecutor or judge to be sympathetic to your arguments.

8

Common Problems in Restoring Firearms Rights

MINOR POST-INCIDENT CONVICTIONS

If you are seeking a pardon or expungement of the record regarding your disqualifying incident, any blot on your criminal history since that time is likely to cause you significant trouble, and there is little you can do about it. Even fish and game violations blow your odds, especially if they are hunting incidents that show you've been using a firearm since the incident. Courts often see repeated speeding tickets as a display of disrespect for the law. Be prepared to have to prove that you are an angel.

If your record is not angelic, see if it is possible to expunge any of the other items on your record before going after the larger disqualifying incident. Alternatively, make sure that the positive information about you drastically outweighs the bad stuff. Another alternative is simply to wait and keep your nose clean in the meantime. The farther in the past the troublesome incidents appear, the better your odds of convincing a court or prosecutor that miscreant behavior is all behind you. A good rule of thumb is that courts like to see 10 years elapsed without criminal incident between the time you have been released from your most recent probation to the time you apply for pardon or expungement.

INABILITY TO OBTAIN OLD CRIMINAL RECORDS

Many states have a system of destroying old criminal convictions, particularly records of misdemeanors, after a certain period of time. This creates difficulty either in proving that your conviction was for a misdemeanor, not a felony, or in obtaining a pardon or expungement where you must provide records of your conviction.

If the state in which you have a conviction destroys misdemeanor records, try to get certification from a record keeper that the record was destroyed and therefore was a misdemeanor record. I've had good luck doing this in several East Coast states.

If the state or local court system doesn't have an established policy of destroying records but claims they can't find them, you may want to spend the money to hire a private investigator to sit and physically go through the records looking for the material you need. Often these records are in voluminous, manually indexed or unindexed boxes, and the record keepers just don't want (or have the time and funds) to go looking for it.

If your Brady denial was on the grounds that you have a felony conviction—but you know your conviction was actually for a misdemeanor—if you cannot find your records, you can try finding a certifiable copy of the version of the statute you were convicted under at the time of your conviction. I had success with this method by locating a decades-old version of a Florida statute demonstrating that operating a vehicle without the owner's consent (joyriding) was a misdemeanor at the time my client was convicted, even though it is a felony today.

You can usually find at least a portion of the records. If the court file does not exist, see if you can at least get a certified copy of the docket sheet or clerk's index. In some states there is a separate file of clerk's or judge's notes; getting these may mean finding the individual clerk or judge from your case.

DIFFICULTY LOCATING MILITARY RECORDS

If there is a question in regard to a military conviction, hospitalization, or discharge, your best possible option is to seek the assistance of your congressional representative's office. These folks' constituent service staff can work miracles. Even so, military records can be very difficult to obtain. If they don't want to give you yours, you may be up a creek without the proverbial paddle, as civil courts have limited powers to deal with military records issues. You might try sending the relative branch of the service a Freedom of Information Act request for your records.

If you were in the armed services around the time of your disqualifying conviction, it may be worth exploring whether the original conviction can be attacked on the basis of the Soldiers and Sailors Relief Act. This federal statute provides certain safeguards to members of the military, given the practical reality that military personnel who are ordered to another base or shipped off to war clearly can't also be in court on a date they've been summoned. If you were on active duty at the time of the conviction or at the time a warrant was issued against you, you have a good chance of having it declared invalid.

FEDERAL CONVICTIONS

Nearly all of the tips and techniques outlined above were focused on convictions in state courts. If you were convicted in federal court, you will have a more difficult row to hoe. Federal court felonies all "count" for purposes of Brady prohibition, and federal felony convictions can only be removed by presidential pardon. The good news on federal convictions is that the record of whether something is a felony or misdemeanor is usually clear, and if there has been a mistake in identity or an error in calling something a felony, the records are generally more easily available than they may be in state court.

With federal convictions, be particularly careful to research the statute you were convicted under at the time of conviction. Congress has been leading the nation in increasing the ramifications and penalties for federal crimes, and it may be that the statute you were convicted under could be construed as a misdemeanor at the time of your charges.

9

Worst-Case Scenarios:
ATF Seizure or Criminal Charges

WHAT IF THE ATF COMES FOR MY GUNS?

In each of the last several years, Congress has appropriated significant funds for additional ATF agents and prosecutors to handle gun prosecutions. Congress has even expanded the exemptions to the Posse Comitatus Act of 1878 and allowed for supportive military roles in drug or firearms criminal cases, so if you are under investigation for a firearms law violation, you may not be imagining those black helicopters circling around your house.

In keeping with the adage to be careful what you wish for, many firearms owners who urged that we "enforce the gun laws we already have" now find that requested enforcement at their doorsteps. Within a few days of receiving a Brady denial, ATF agents are likely to appear and request that you "voluntarily" give them your guns. The agents may suggest that if you are cooperative, you might not be criminally prosecuted. They sometimes threaten immediate arrest if you do not cooperate.

You have an absolute right to not speak to the ATF agents, and it is sound legal advice to refuse to do so. You have an absolute right to refuse them entry to your home and to decline to turn over your firearms or any other possessions if they do not have a warrant. You have a right to have an attorney present if you choose to turn over the firearms. It is wise to immediately telephone an attorney and have him or her on the phone or, if possible, present during any interaction you have with the ATF. Assuming that you are reasonably polite, it is unclear whether your capitulation will have any effect on whether you will be prosecuted; it would also be unusual that ATF would have grounds for your immediate arrest unless a federal indictment has already been issued.

A good course to follow if ATF arrives at your door is to:

1. Ask to see any warrant or indictment they may have, as well as their badges or other identification;
2. Advise the agents to wait on your doorstep while you telephone an attorney;
3. Determine with the attorney whether it is in your best interest at that time to hand over any firearms in your possession;
4. If so, either turn over the firearms at your doorstep or clearly state to the agents where in your home you are permitting them to be (you may hand this statement to them in writing, or have another person run a video camera during your discussion with the agents), and insist on a complete receipt, signed and dated by the agents, including all firearms' makes, models, and serial numbers. Remember that it is lawful to possess gun cases, slings, holsters, and optics; you may wish to remove these items from any guns surrendered to at least minimize any economic loss.

CRIMINAL CHARGES

The most common criminal charge arising out of a Brady denial is a charge of federal felony perjury where the applicant has falsely stated on ATF Form 4473 that he is not guilty of a felony or a misdemeanor crime of domestic violence, or does not have some other disqualification, when in fact the applicant has the conviction or other disqualification. A Brady denial can trigger investigation into whether the applicant already owns other firearms, in which case he can be charged with felony unlawful possession of a firearm. That investigation can include checking with local police and game wardens, looking for state or local firearms licenses, and checking fish and game records to determine if the applicant has reported game taken during rifle or shotgun seasons.

Being arrested or receiving a criminal citation for a federal felony is a very serious event. If you are in this position, it is urgent that you contact an attorney before making any substantive statements whatsoever to law enforcement authorities. Most criminal convictions are based at least in large part on the statements of the person being charged with the crime. Explaining will not help, except to dig yourself further into trouble. The only information you should impart to law enforcement at your arrest is your correct name, date of birth, address, and any minimal information necessary to avoid what may be a life-or-death situation (for instance, if you are at risk because you require medications, or if you know someone else may be at immediate risk, such as when in your haste to get your firearms out of the house, you dumped them in an elementary school play yard).

You will not be able to assess your options rationally in the moments of stress and emotional fury surrounding being arrested. Lawyer up and stay calm and focused so that you will be able to make the best choices for yourself as to how to proceed once additional information about your charges and position can be obtained.

10

Looking Ahead

HOW CAN I SAFEGUARD MY RIGHT TO BEAR ARMS?

Learn and exercise your rights *and fulfill your citizenship duties* under your state and federal constitutions. That means taking an active role in your government. Vote. Run for office. Work on campaigns for candidates who share your views. Democracy is a full-contact sport, not a spectator sport.

Do not try to safeguard firearms rights by trammeling other constitutionally protected rights. Some people suggest that "lawful gun owners" will benefit by doing away with rights of trial by jury or the right of bail for "criminals." Don't forget that the gun rights we hold so dear were secured by our forefathers, who were religious dissidents, rum-runners, smugglers, and rioters who committed armed treason against their king. Is it any wonder that they deemed safeguards on the criminal trial process to be as important as arms?

Assess new criminal law and law enforcement authority laws critically, and let your congressmen and state legislators know your thoughts in writing and through testimony in any public hearings held before these laws are adopted.

Don't be complacent. When the Brady Act was passed, most firearms owners were silent. Hunters believed Brady would not affect their rifles and shotguns; now it does. People who did not consider themselves "criminals" believed it would never impact them, but many people with no criminal history have been victims of typing errors that can only be corrected with time, expense, and stress.

Firearms owners were also mostly silent when the amendment went through in 1998 adding the prohibition for misdemeanor crimes of domestic violence. It's hard to publicly argue with the idea of taking guns away from people who beat their wives—but in fact, this prohibition applies to many people who were involved in very minor family disputes; if their cases had involved serious assault, the prosecutor would have charged them as felonies.

Opening the door to attaching felony-type punishments to one misdemeanor crime means that Congress can do so to other misdemeanor crimes. I would not be at all surprised to see future firearms prohibitions for misdemeanor drug crimes (like possessing a joint in 1967), misdemeanor crimes of violence (like disorderly conduct), or misdemeanor weapons crimes (like shooting a deer with antlers that were too short). The public relations people will say "Gee, you don't want drug dealers having guns, do you? Or violent criminals? Or people who have already committed crimes with weapons?" But the fact is, once they get to that point, they will have removed the guns from the majority of people in the country.

Most people who have a criminal conviction are somewhat embarrassed about it, or think of themselves as unusual for having a criminal record. While the statistics on this are impossible to prove, if you include all the traffic and fish and game violations and all the domestic restraining orders, the vast majority of the adult public has some kind of criminal conviction on their record. It is, in fact, the norm—and when you talk about taking guns out of the hands of criminals, you are talking about taking the guns away from most of us.

In some demographic groups of United States citizens, this fact is painfully obvious. The United States has the highest incarceration rate in the world, and for certain populations it is so high it is shocking. Based on the incarceration and disenfranchisement rates for black men in the United States, I estimate that well over half of all adult black men in the United States are prohibited from possessing firearms. In Vermont, based on criminal conviction statistics and information from our criminal records center, I estimate that one in three adult men in the state are prohibited from possessing firearms by federal law—and this in a state that prides itself on its firearms ownership. Taking guns out of the hands of criminals means an awful lot of us. Don't presume that these gun control laws won't affect you.

Support all firearms rights, not just those you think won't apply inside your living room. And support all the other rights guaranteed to all citizens under state and U.S. constitutions. They are all interconnected and equally important.

Never trade your liberty for the illusion of safety or security. You are the sovereign power of your state and the United States. Do not surrender your right to govern yourself, or let that right be stolen from you because it seems easier to let someone else do the hard work of governing. You, the citizen, are the sovereign of this country, and your right to bear arms is an important element of that sovereignty.

The question of who is or is not prohibited from possessing firearms under the gun control statutes and the Brady Act is not the clear-cut, easily supportable issue that the media and Congress seem to think it is. With careful planning and a lot of work you can overturn your Brady denial and restore your firearms rights.

APPENDIX

Resources

REGULATIONS OF THE BUREAU OF ALCOHOL, TOBACCO, FIREARMS, AND EXPLOSIVES

The ATF regulations regarding firearms sales and possessions are found in *The Code of Federal Regulations*, Volume 27 Chapter II beginning at section 447. The FBI's NICS regulations regarding Brady denial appeals are found at the *Code of Federal Regulations*, Volume 28 Chapter I beginning at Section 25. *The Code of Federal Regulations* can be found online at any number of law library and government Web sites and should be available in a print version at any library that serves as a government documents repository. The *Federal Register*, usually shelved right next to *The Code of Federal Regulations*, publishes all proposed new regulations of all the federal agencies and notes how you may submit comments on proposed regulations before they are adopted.

STATE LAWS AND PUBLISHED ORDINANCES—FIREARMS

The ATF publishes its annual volume of state firearms laws, revised every year. It is ATF publication number 53000.5. You can purchase a copy from the Superintendent of Documents, U.S. Government Printing Office, Washington, D.C. 20402.

FINDING A FIREARMS LAWYER

Most state bar association referral services do not have a special category of firearms attorneys; however, the National Rifle Association maintains a referral list of attorneys practicing in the firearms law field in every state.

If you call the NRA for a referral to an attorney in your state, ask if any of the attorneys listed specify that they represent people on Brady denials. The reason for this is that most "firearms law" involves defending people against fish and game violations, criminal charges involving firearms, or product liability suits. If none of the attorneys on the list in your state say they practice Brady denial law, you may still try calling the other attorneys on the NRA referral list for a recommendation.

Another good source would be your local shooting or sportsmen's clubs, many of which have attorneys as members or have legal counsel for the organization.

Most Brady denial appeals are less about firearms than they are about criminal history records. If you cannot find a firearms lawyer who practices Brady denial law, your next best bet is a criminal defense attorney, especially one who handles appeals. Appellate criminal defense attorneys can usually be found through your state bar association referral service.

Sample Request for Reasons for Denial Letter

Jimmy Gunowner
123 Anystreet, Apartment 2B
Yourtown, Yourstate 12345

15 January 2006

Federal Bureau of Investigation
NICS Section
Appeals Services Team Module A-1
P.O. Box 4278
Clarksburg, WV 26302-9922

RE: NTN # 49385-JK
REQUEST FOR REASON FOR DENIAL

Dear Sir or Madam,

On 12 January 2006, I attempted to purchase a firearm at Joe's Gun Shop, located in Yourtown, Yourstate. After completing Form 4473 and providing the necessary identification, I was advised by Joe, the FFL, that my Brady background check resulted in a Denial from NICS.

I hereby request that you provide me, in writing, with a statement of the reason for that denial. I

have enclosed my fingerprint 10 card in the hopes
that this might expeditiously resolve this matter.

Thank you for your prompt attention. I understand
that you must respond to this request within five
business days of its receipt.

Very truly yours,

Jimmy Gunowner
enc. Fingerprint card

Sample Administrative Brady Appeal Letter

Jimmy Gunowner
123 Anystreet, Apartment 2B
Yourtown, Yourstate 12345

15 February 2006

Federal Bureau of Investigation
NICS Operations Center
Criminal Justice Information Services Division
1000 Custer Hollow Road Module C-3
Clarksburg, WV 26306-0147

RE: NTN # 49385-JK
Appeal from Denial of Firearms Transaction

Dear Sir or Madam,
On 12 January 2006, I attempted to purchase a firearm at Joe's Gun Shop, located in Yourtown, Yourstate. After completing Form 4473 and providing the necessary identification, I was advised by Joe, the FFL, that my Brady background check resulted in a Denial from NICS.

On 15 January 2005 I wrote to your Appeals Services Team as directed in the Code of Federal Regulations, requesting the reason for the

denial. On 22 January 2006 I received the statement of reasons, a copy of which is attached. The
reason stated is a felony DUI conviction received
on May 19, 1945, in the state of South Carolina.
I hereby appeal the Brady denial issued on 12
January 2005 for reasons including, but not limited to, that stated below.

GROUNDS FOR APPEAL

The stated reason for denial of my attempted
firearms transaction is erroneous. I was born on
May 19, 1954, nine years after the alleged DUI conviction. The conviction referenced in the statement
of reasons for denial bears a name similar to mine
but cannot be, and is not, my conviction.

I have enclosed a certified copy of my birth certificate together with my fingerprint 10 card in
the hopes that this might expeditiously resolve
this matter.
Thank you for your prompt attention.

Very truly yours,

Jimmy Gunowner
enc. Fingerprint card,
certified copy of birth certificate.

Glossary

ATF Form 4473—This form must be completed to begin a Brady check. It asks questions about the purchaser's identity and criminal history and other information relative to the firearms statutes. Providing false information on this form is considered perjury.

ATF—The Bureau of Alcohol, Tobacco, Firearms, and Explosives.

The Brady Handgun Violence Prevention Act of 1993—The act requires FFLs to request background checks on anyone attempting to purchase a firearm. It is named for White House Press Secretary James S. Brady, who was injured in the 1981 attempted assassination of President Ronald Reagan.

CLEO—Chief Law Enforcement Officer. Before NICS, the law enforcement officers in an applicant's town determined the potential gun buyer's Brady status.

FFL—Federal Firearms License. Refers to a dealer with the certification to sell firearms.

NICS—National Instant Check System. An FBI entity that may be called by the FFL to obtain permission to sell a firearm to a specific customer. See also POC.

NICS AST—The NICS Appeals Services Team responds to your request for the reasons for your denial and sends a statement of reasons in writing. If the denial is related to your criminal history, you will usually receive a copy of the criminal record indicating the date, conviction, and the charging agency.

NTN—NICS Transaction Number. The number assigned your case for the denial of a specific firearm purchase.

POC—Point of Contact. A state agency that is the federally authorized point of contact for FFLs calling in a request to sell a firearm. See also NICS.

TRO—Temporary Restraining Order. A restraining order issued in domestic abuse cases. The terminology varies from state to state, and it may also be called an abuse prevention order or a family court stay-away order.

About the Author

Cindy Ellen Hill has been engaged in the practice of firearms and criminal defense law in Massachusetts and Vermont for 20 years. An enthusiastic sports shooter and antique-gun collector, she has assisted clients to successfully overturn dozens of Brady denials and advises attorneys in other states on hundreds more. She lives with her family in Middlebury, Vermont.